THE STORY OF
THE TYNESIDE SCOTTISH

Colonel Joseph Cowen.
(Donor of £15,000).

[*Frontispiece.*

THE STORY OF THE TYNESIDE SCOTTISH

By
Brigadier-General TREVOR TERNAN
C.B., C.M.G., D.S.O.

THE NORTHUMBERLAND PRESS,
WATERLOO HOUSE, THORNTON STREET,
NEWCASTLE-UPON-TYNE.

DEDICATED
To
THE FIGHTING FIFTH
(THE NORTHUMBERLAND FUSILIERS)

TO WHICH GREAT REGIMENT
THE TYNESIDE SCOTTISH HAS THE HONOUR TO BELONG

FOREWORD

By

FIELD-MARSHAL SIR DOUGLAS HAIG
K.T., O.M., G.C.B., G.C.M.G., G.C.V.O.,
Commander-in-Chief of the British Expeditionary Force in France and Flanders.

The story of gallant actions recorded in this book bears more eloquent testimony to the courage and devotion of the "Tyneside Scottish" than any I can give. I am glad, however, to pay my personal tribute to a hard working and hard fighting Brigade that did most splendid service on many an occasion.

(Signed) D. HAIG,
Field-Marshal.

CONTENTS

CHAP.		PAGE
	FOREWORD	3
	WARNING	7
I.	FORMATION OF BRIGADE	9
II.	TRAINING AT ALNWICK	17
III.	THE BRIGADE AT LONGBRIDGE DEVERILL	23
IV.	DEPARTURE FOR FRANCE	29
V.	A VISIT TO THE FRONT LINE TRENCHES	33
VI.	AN UNOFFICIAL INSPECTION	40
VII.	THE BRIGADE TAKES OVER A PORTION OF THE LINE	47
VIII.	CAMOUFLAGE MADE A FINE ART	56
IX.	THE TRENCH "GARRISONS"	63
X.	THE TRENCH MORTAR BATTERIES	70
XI.	THE BRIGADE HEADQUARTERS AT THE VILLA ROCHERS	82
XII.	THE ROAR OF A BOMBARDMENT	95
XIII.	THE MEMORABLE 1ST JULY	104
XIV.	AT VIMY RIDGE	114
XV.	THE WORK OF RAIDING PARTIES	121
XVI.	SPIES IN THE BRITISH LINES	131
XVII.	THE RIGOURS OF WINTER	139
XVIII.	BATTLE OF ARRAS	151

LIST OF ILLUSTRATIONS

Colonel Joseph Cowen	*Frontispiece*
Officers, 1st Tyneside Scottish	*To face p.* 10
Tyneside Scottish Committee	,, 14
Officers, 2nd Tyneside Scottish	,, 21
On Salisbury Plain	,, 24
Officers, 4th Tyneside Scottish	,, 26
Officers, 3rd Tyneside Scottish	,, 31
Brigade Staff	,, 34
Pipers	,, 44
Portraits	,, 52-54
A Village in France	,, 70
The Cathedral—Albert, 1916	,, 80
La Boisselle	,, 84
Our Ridge at Albert	,, 106
Railway Cutting—Arras	,, 150

WARNING

FRIENDS, especially those back from the war, so frequently in the course of conversation say nice things about the Tyneside Scottish and their great doings in France, and have so often suggested that I should write a " History " of the Brigade, that I have come to the conclusion that though a real " History " would be quite beyond my capabilities and must be left to a more competent writer to compile, still I might perhaps venture to jot down a few odds and ends which would possibly be of interest to past and present members of the Brigade. I should also (and married men will understand that this is no inadequate reason) in this way satisfy to some extent the extortionate demands of my wife and small son, to whom there is of course one Brigade only in the British Army, and of the doings of that Brigade they can never have enough. Should it therefore happen that my scribbling should come to the notice of a larger circle than that composed of my own family, though this does indeed seem to me to be extremely improbable, I would ask the reader for his own sake to pause before proceeding further or to make up his mind to be satisfied with very light fare.

THE STORY OF THE TYNESIDE SCOTTISH

CHAPTER I

FORMATION OF BRIGADE

WELL, to make some sort of a beginning I must go back to the month of December, 1914. I was at that time Assistant Adjutant and Quartermaster-General on the Staff of the Northumbrian Territorial Division, Newcastle-on-Tyne, under the command of Major-General B. Burton, C.B., late R.A., having as an officer of the " Reserve of Officers " been so appointed on the outbreak of war. In short I was a " Dugout," having retired as Brigadier-General in the year 1907.

On 16th December I was informed by wire from London that I had been appointed a Brigadier-General to command one of the new Army local Brigades which were to be formed, and that my Brigade was to be the " Tyneside Scottish." At that time, though it was known in the Divisional office that local Battalions were being formed in Newcastle, little was known on the subject. My orders were to take up my new appointment as soon as my successor arrived, but I eventually prevailed upon my General to let me go without waiting for my successor's arrival. It was not, however, until the 28th December that I was free. In the interval I had lost no time in visiting the local authorities and getting into touch with the Tyneside Scottish Committee, and its indefatigable

Honorary Secretary, Mr J. R. Hall, who gave me full information regarding the four Battalions which were being raised, and which were to form the Brigade, and which were billeted in and about Newcastle. Among other things it was, of course, necessary to arrange for a Brigade office, and also for a temporary Brigade Staff. No. 18 Eskdale Terrace was accordingly rented and furnished as an office by the Tyneside Scottish Committee, and Second-Lieutenant J. H. Patterson, of the 4th Battalion, was appointed temporarily acting staff officer. This young officer was quite inexperienced in military matters and had no knowledge of the duties of a staff officer, but on the other hand was an expert typist and full of zeal. (He was, to my great regret, subsequently killed in France.) Captain Wallace Marrs, of the 2nd Battalion, was lent to me temporarily by his commanding officer to act as Staff Captain, and about a fortnight later Captain T. Soutry, R.I.R., a regular officer who had been wounded in the retreat from Mons, arrived to take up the appointment of Brigade Major. The Battalions which were to form the Brigade were as follows, and were, with the exception of the 4th Battalion, commanded by ex-regular officers:

- The 1st Tyneside Scottish (20th N.F.) by Lieutenant-Colonel C. H. Innes Hopkins (late Scottish Rifles).
- The 2nd Tyneside Scottish (21st N.F.) by Colonel V. M. Stockley (Indian Cavalry).
- The 3rd Tyneside Scottish (22nd N.F.) by Lieutenant-Colonel A. P. A. Elphinstone (Indian Infantry).
- The 4th Tyneside Scottish (23rd N.F.) by Captain J. C. Campbell (Militia).

The Battalions were at this stage very busy at their various centres recruiting, drilling, and getting their uniforms, etc. The 3rd Battalion was quartered at Newburn, the 4th at Gosforth, the

FORMATION OF BRIGADE

1st and 2nd in and near Newcastle. The whole of the work of supplying the large amount of military clothing and equipment required, as well as the rationing and billeting of the Battalions was, at the request of the War Office, carried out by the Lord Mayor, who entrusted the duty to a responsible and representative committee, and well they did it. Their efforts embraced not only the requirements of the Tyneside Scottish but of the Tyneside Irish Brigade, and were entirely successful. On looking back to that time one can only wonder at the marvellous success of the work of these energetic, patriotic men who, in the absence of any adequate War Office organisation, threw themselves into the gap, so to speak, and successfully raised, clothed, and equipped the Brigades, and thus enabled at least 10,000 local men to take the field.

To revert to the Brigade. Drilling was being carried out in side streets in Newcastle, and in the most unlikely places, the majority of the men being in plain clothes. The men in those days were all keen volunteers, most of them miners, a large proportion of whom were married men with families. It was soon evident that here was in my hands all the material for a magnificent Brigade, the physique of the men, after the necessary weeding out of the "crocks" had been attended to, left nothing to be desired, and I quickly came to the conclusion that though the bulk of the officers had had little or no previous military experience, their keenness to learn, and intelligence would soon rectify that matter. Nor was I wrong, as events proved. My very high estimate of the value of the officers and men was subsequently only too fully demonstrated, as I will describe in its proper place to the best of my ability. What did puzzle me very much at first was the "Tyneside speech." Many a time when attempting to talk to a man in the ranks I knocked up against a, to me, perfectly unintelligible reply, and I must confess that in spite of my best endeavours, though I improved to some extent, I

Lieut.-Colonel C. H. Innes-Hopkins and Officers,
1st. Batt. Tyneside Scottish, 1915.

[To face p. 10.

have never yet reached any degree of proficiency in the language of the Tyne. I know it has its admirers, and no doubt it deserves admiration; I refrain from expressing an opinion. When the request was made by Lord Kitchener for the raising of these local Battalions the regulations required that the Lord Mayor should be responsible for the finance, and although the government was expected to make good to the local authorities all the expenditure incurred according to vocabulary rates in connection with the raising, rationing, housing, clothing, and equipping of the new local troops, it was recognised that before successful results could be achieved, funds which admitted of a more elastic expenditure were required.

The Tyneside Brigade's Fund was therefore initiated by a gift of £10,000, afterwards increased to £15,000, from Colonel Joseph Cowen, of Stella Hall, which sum was to be devoted to such expenditure on behalf of these locally raised troops as could not be met out of Government funds. The fund was placed in the hands and at the discretion of the two trustees, Mr Johnstone Wallace (now Colonel Sir Johnstone Wallace, K.B.E.), who as Lord Mayor of Newcastle, in 1914, was the " raiser " of the local Brigades, and Colonel Joseph Reed, of Horton Grange, Dudley. Under the wise administration of these gentlemen this fund has proved invaluable to the troops, and it is unnecessary to say how greatly Colonel Cowen's magnificent gift has been appreciated. The liability of the trustees reached nearly £100,000 before there were any reimbursements from the Government, and their total ultimate expenditure exceeded £500,000 before the Brigades were taken over by the War Office. At this period it was necessary for me to frequently visit the various Battalions and their detachments, and I often found myself at Newburn, a few miles up the Tyne from Newcastle, where the 3rd Battalion was billeted. They were lucky in having at their disposal for drilling pur-

FORMATION OF BRIGADE

poses a considerable piece of ground on the right bank of the river. At Newcastle itself the town moor was placed at the disposal of the Battalions billeted there, and at Gosforth a small field was available for the use of the 4th Battalion, but it was evident that the wide distribution of the Brigade, and the absence of any really suitable training ground was very deliterious to progress, so that when it was known that the construction of a large hutment camp was contracted for and was being built in the Duke of Northumberland's Park at Alnwick, there was much rejoicing and some anxiety as to which, if any, of the Battalions of the Tyneside Scottish would be lucky enough to get there. I was naturally very desirous of getting my Brigade concentrated in camp somewhere, and the possibility of a camp at Alnwick seemed almost too good to be true.

It was eventually decided, to my great satisfaction, that the Brigade should be concentrated at Alnwick, and accordingly the 1st Battalion left Newcastle on 29th January, 1915, by march route, halting for the night at Morpeth, arriving at Alnwick the next day. The Brigade Headquarters moved on 1st March, 1915, and the 2nd Battalion followed on the 12th March. The whole Brigade was concentrated in Alnwick shortly afterwards. I have always looked upon this concentration of the Brigade in such a perfect camp as a huge stroke of fortune, and as the main factor resulting beyond any other in the undoubtedly very high standard of training and discipline to which the Brigade so rapidly attained. Officers and men had most comfortable accommodation in magnificent surroundings, and the facilities for training left nothing to be desired. Steady drill was carried out in the park, a range for musketry was available within three or four miles, and later on the extensive moors in the neighbourhood provided ample room for digging trenches and carrying out schemes for "attack" and "defence." It was at Alnwick that the foundations of the Brigade were laid. It was during this time that both officers and men gradually and unconsciously grew out of individualism and came to look upon themselves as something more than detached men; they belonged to the brotherhood of the Tyneside Scots, a truly proud and noble brotherhood as events proved.

I do not think I am wrong in estimating that it was due to the zeal and devotion of both officers and men during their period of training at Alnwick that their success in the field in France was originally due. Life at Alnwick, however, was not all work. There was plenty of opportunity for amusement in the way of gymkhanas, sports, and concerts. Men also were able to take an occasional week-end leave to their homes. The Brigade which was originally known as the 123rd Infantry Brigade now became the 102nd. I have no notes at my disposal, so that exact dates can in few instances be given, but it was, I believe, some time in May, 1915, that the Brigade was inspected by his Grace the Duke of Northumberland, K.G., as Lord-Lieutenant of the County. The parade was attended by Sir Thomas Oliver, Chairman of the Tyneside Scottish Committee and Honorary Colonel of the 1st Battalion, Mr Johnstone Wallace, Colonel J. Reed (Honorary Colonel of the 2nd Battalion), and other members of the Committee. The whole party, including a number of the senior officers and their wives, subsequently lunched as guests of the Tyneside Brigade's Committee at an hotel in Alnwick, where a number of eulogistic speeches were made expressing the entire confidence of the gathering in the future of the Brigade. It was shortly after this that orders were received that the Brigade was to take part in a parade of troops on the Town Moor at Newcastle to be held on 20th May, 1915, for review by his Majesty the King. The Brigade was accordingly railed to Newcastle for the occasion. His Majesty, who on this occasion reviewed a force of about 18,000

J. R. HALL, ESQ.

MAJOR E. E. McCLINTOCK.

(Joint Hon. Secretaries).

COL. W. M. ANGUS, C.B.

LORD ARMSTRONG.
Vice Chairman of Committee.

PROF. J WIGHT DUFF.

J. T. STEELE, ESQ.

ANGUS WATSON, ESQ.
(Chairman of Dependents' Com.).

SOME MEMBERS OF THE TYNESIDE SCOTTISH COMMITTEE.

[*To face p.* 14.

FORMATION OF BRIGADE

troops, rode slowly along the front of each Brigade, and was graciously pleased to express to me his great satisfaction at the extremely soldierly appearance of the Tyneside Scottish. It was on this occasion that his Majesty suggested that it would be an improvement if our " Glengarries " could be replaced by " Balmorals," as the latter afforded much better shade to the eyes, and requested Lord Kitchener, who accompanied his Majesty, to see if such a change could be made. I was accordingly directed by Lord Kitchener to send in the necessary indents at once. This I did on the following day, but it was not till many months later that the " Balmorals " actually materialised. Up to the time of the review by his Majesty, though some hundreds of rifles had been issued to each Battalion for instructional purposes, a complete supply of arms had not been made to the Brigade. The authorities got over this difficulty temporarily by sending us several thousand old pattern rifles to be used on this parade only so that we should present a uniform appearance. These rifles which it was alleged, probably untruthfully, had originally come from the Tower of London had been used by other troops just before on a similar occasion, and as our men had been trained to handle service rifles they answered the purpose admirably. After the parade the rifles were despatched immediately to Stirling to meet a similar emergency.

A little later Major-General Lawson, C.B., the G.O.C. Northern Command, carried out an inspection of the Brigade, and expressed himself as well satisfied with the bearing and steadiness of the men on parade. Though we saw little of any representative of the outside military world at Alnwick we were not forgotten and correspondence was heavy, and the day came when the A.S.C. took over the task of feeding us, a duty which had been hitherto so admirably carried out by the Committee, and we were also gradually supplied with our transport. We received orders about this time that we were to form part of the 34th Division, which comprised two other infantry Brigades, one of which was the 101st and the other the 103rd, our old friends and rivals the Tyneside Irish Brigade. The Division was commanded by Major-General C. Ingouville-Williams, C.B., who had distinguished himself as a Brigadier in the early days of the war in France. He paid us a visit of inspection, I think in June, and after making a careful inspection of the camp, expressed himself as surprised and greatly pleased at the soldierly appearance and turn-out of the men. He expressed himself also as much struck by the smartness of the various guards and sentries which he passed, and the extreme neatness of the camp.

CHAPTER II

TRAINING AT ALNWICK

SOON after the formation of the Brigade orders were received from the Northern Command, with whom until the formation of the 34th Division the Brigade was in direct communication, that the 12th Battalion East Yorks Regiment was attached to my Brigade for training and discipline. This Battalion was under the capable command of Lieutenant-Colonel F. W. Becher, and was very comfortably quartered in a large country house not far from Middlesbrough, the grounds of which were ample for steady drill purposes. Though I did manage to pay one or two visits to Middlesbrough the supervision I could exercise as regards the training was merely nominal as my hands were full nearer home. There was, however, the usual amount of official correspondence between the Battalion and the Brigade office, which continued until we left Alnwick in August, when the attachment of the Battalion to the Brigade ceased. This Battalion was composed of such excellent material and was shaping so well that I am sure it must have distinguished itself in the field. I have often wondered in which Division it found itself, and in which theatre of war.

Of course in the case of an entirely new organisation such as the Tyneside Scottish Brigade there were a large number of questions constantly cropping up which had to be settled. In all those of a financial nature the solution was simple owing to the remarkable generosity of the Cowen Fund and numerous friends of the Brigade. For instance, each Battalion was allowed by regulation the personnel of a small pipe band, and in each case the sets of pipes and the outfits of the pipers were given by friends of the Brigade. When one considers that a complete outfit for a piper cost, I believe, even in those days not less than £30, the generosity of the donors can be estimated. In the case of the 1st Battalion Colonel C. H. Innes Hopkins, to whom the Battalion is in many ways so deeply indebted, equipped his band at his own expense, and selected as tartan a modest black and white check. The other Battalions were ambitious and boldly adopted the tartans of well-known Highland clans, each a different one. Though I am now, and was then, acutely aware of my entire ignorance of the subject of tartans I always felt the unauthorised use of other people's tartans must be unsound, and I therefore suggested that the Brigade should institute a tartan of its own. This course having been agreed to by C.O.'s the question as to the pattern had to be decided, and eventually one was submitted which met with the approval of the C.O.'s and became the Brigade tartan.

While this tartan has no particular claims to beauty, in fact, I have heard it described in no very complimentary terms, it has at least the merit of being quiet and unassuming, and is quite free from the somewhat defiant note to be sometimes found in the more old established brands. Then there was the question of the cap badge. The badge in use by the Brigade though neat was, it was thought, somewhat too small and insignificant, and it was decided that one of a rather more pronounced Scottish as well as Tyneside character would be desirable. Several patterns of badges were submitted, and one designed by a junior officer of the 4th Battalion, was at last selected.

On Sunday, the 10th of January, 1915, a parade took place in the Haymarket, Newcastle, after which the 2,000 men attended a special service in St Nicholas Cathedral, and a very able sermon

TRAINING AT ALNWICK

was preached by the Vicar of Newcastle, Canon Gough. I have no doubt that this service made a vivid impression on the minds of those who attended; it was in effect a "blessing" of the Brigade by the Church, and was felt by many to be an encouragement and incentive in their efforts. It was not until a later date that chaplains of various denominations were appointed, but eventually we had attached to the Brigade two Church of England, one Roman Catholic, and one Nonconformist chaplains, all good men with their hearts in their work. The Rev. Father J. McHardy, the Roman Catholic chaplain, subsequently gained the Military Cross for gallantry under fire.

During the time the Brigade was at Alnwick the Church of England services were conducted in camp, the Brigade being drawn up in hollow square on the grassy slope between the camp and the river. The dignified ancient Castle on the opposite slope of the little valley formed a rare background to the scene, and it would indeed be difficult to find more beautiful surroundings for a service than those afforded by the greenery of the park, with its magnificent timber, the sparkling little river, and the view of the Castle which dominated the landscape. On fine days a certain number of townsfolk and friends of officers and men in the Brigade attended these services, and evidently enjoyed them, as well as watching the march past after the service of the different Battalions headed by their pipe bands, each piper bent on getting every ounce of martial music out of his instrument. There was great rivalry between the bands, which in those days were largely composed of especially enlisted trained pipers, proud indeed of their skill and determined to make a brave show at the head of their Battalion. How truly gallant a body these pipers were was abundantly proved later. The majority fell at La Boisselle on the 1st July, 1916, and the pipes in which they took such pride, and played with their last breaths, were lost or now only exist as torn and bloody fragments reverently preserved as treasured relics of that band of heroes, the " Tyneside Scottish Pipers."

The Lord Mayor of Newcastle was at this time Alderman John Fitzgerald, who had succeeded Colonel Johnstone Wallace in November, 1914, and, in addition to his usual hospitalities, he inaugurated a series of banquets at the Mansion House in honour of the various locally raised bodies. To these banquets Mr Fitzgerald invited the members of the various Committees interested in the formation of the Brigade concerned, and the senior officers of each Brigade. Mr Fitzgerald's hospitality was prodigious. It was a pleasure on these occasions to listen to the really excellent speeches made both by himself and the members of the Committee. To a stranger like myself it was most interesting to listen to the recital of the steps taken by Committees or individuals which gradually resulted in the magnificently successful local recruiting movement. The speakers in many cases hardly seemed to be aware of the significance of their efforts and the immense results attained. It was all, apparently, regarded as merely part of the day's work. It was Lord Kitchener's wish that the local authorities in Newcastle should obtain recruits and raise local Brigades, and they obtained the recruits and raised the Brigades accordingly. In reality this work was no such simple job; it was in fact a splendid feat. I have no doubt that later generations will look back with pride upon those virile energetic ancestors of theirs, whose zeal, capacity, and success in a time of grave national stress were so remarkably demonstrated.

In addition to the official hospitality of the Mansion House, much private entertaining of officers and men was carried out by friends, Sir Thomas Oliver and Colonel Joseph Reed being much to the fore in this connection. On one occasion, I think it was after the Church service at the Cathedral previously referred to, these gentle-

Lieut.-Colonel Dunbar Stuart and Officers,
2nd Batt. Tyneside Scottish, 1915.

TRAINING AT ALNWICK

men organised a tea to several hundreds of men of the Battalions of which they were Honorary Colonels, and on another occasion the manager of one of the theatres gave a free entertainment to one of the Battalions.

All this time under the energetic guidance of their commanding officers the Battalions were progressing rapidly. There were so many subjects to be taught and, as we then thought, so little time at our disposal that every hour was of value. I think we all hoped, and expected, that we should find ourselves in France in August or September at the latest. Instruction in all sorts of subjects, such as musketry, signalling, machine gunnery, telephones, camp sanitation, transport, had all been feverishly pushed on. It was a time indeed of intensive training. Route marching, trench digging, relief of trenches, outposts' attack and defence were all liberally practised by day and by night, and by July we felt that we were really ready to meet the Boches. The discipline and moral of the men were excellent and their physique splendid. They were a truly hard lot. Thanks to the fact that in each Battalion there was available a first-class instructor in signalling, the signallers, all keen to learn, had reached a remarkable degree of proficiency. The transport officers, all men accustomed to horses in civil life, had brought the transport to a high standard. The marching power of the Brigade proved to be excellent. The officers, bright, cheery, and intelligent, had reached a high stage of professional proficiency. The shooting of the Brigade was above the average. The one anxiety of all ranks was to get to France. Thus matters stood in July, 1915.

Since the earlier days some changes among the senior officers of the Brigade had occurred. Colonel V. M. Stockley, who was originally commanding the 2nd Battalion, had been succeeded by Lieutenant-Colonel Dunbar-Stuart, previously the second in command of the 1st Battalion, and

Major E. K. Purnell had been appointed to the command of the 4th Battalion, vice Major Campbell. Captain Wallace Marrs had been confirmed in his appointment of Staff Captain to the Brigade, and Lieutenant E. Turnbull, 1st Battalion, had joined my staff as orderly officer. Second-Lieutenant Patterson had returned to duty with his Battalion. Lieutenant A. P. Ker, of the 1st Battalion, became Brigade transport officer, and a very excellent one he made. It was about this time that we one day received orders that the Brigade was to proceed on a certain early date to Ripon, where the 34th Division was to be concentrated, and the necessary preliminary steps for the move were consequently taken. The Staff Captain was sent down to reconnoitre the accommodation, etc., and the married officers arranged for furnished houses or rooms, the landladies concerned demanding payment in advance. The order to move was, however, subsequently cancelled, and I suppose the only people who were really pleased were certain landladies. Shortly after this, however, fresh orders were received ordering the move of the Brigade to Salisbury Plain, and we accordingly entrained at Alnwick on the 1st August, 1915. The Brigade occupied ten trains, and arrived at Luggershall on the 2nd, where it was accommodated under canvas.

CHAPTER III

THE BRIGADE AT LONGBRIDGE DEVERILL

THE routine at Windmill Hill was very similar to that at Alnwick, except that the Brigade was under canvas instead of in huts. A great deal of time was given up to musketry, bombing practise, and route marching, and one day a week to a Brigade exercise. General Sir Arthur Paget, G.C.B., the G.O.C. in C. Salisbury Plain, inspected the Brigade on parade soon after its arrival. At first the weather was fine, and though all ranks were kept very fully employed, life was pleasant and healthy. Towards the end of September, however, the men began to suffer the first taste of discomfort. Storms of wind and rain at times levelled the tents, and we were not sorry to hear that we were to move shortly into huts at Longbridge Deverill, near Warminster, though we wondered why we could not go direct to France. The move to Longbridge Deverill took place on the 26th September, 1915, the Battalions being railed to Warminster. During our stay at Windmill Hill we had had the pleasure of a visit from Colonel Johnstone Wallace, Colonel Sir Thomas Oliver, and Colonel Joseph Reed, who came down on behalf of the Committee to have a look at us, and find out if there was anything they could do for us. They were accommodated in tents in the Brigade Headquarters' camp, and we did our best to entertain them, but I fear the accommodation and our cuisine was not all that could be desired.

No very outstanding incidents occur to my memory as regards the period at Windmill Hill. We, however, made the closer acquaintance of General Ingouville-Williams, and the Divisional Staff and the other units in the Division. A point very rightly and strongly insisted upon was the smart rendering of compliments by the various sentries and guards to general officers when they rode through the camps, and General Williams was pleased to intimate that our guards and sentries were considered as particularly good. After we had been a very short time at Longbridge Deverill the Infantry of the Division were fully convinced that the unreadiness of the Artillery was the reason for the prolonged detention of the Division in England, and it is possible that this was the case as the training of Artillery takes time. But whatever the reason may have been there is no doubt that about this time all ranks of the Tyneside Scottish began to think that they were being unduly delayed at home, and a certain feeling of staleness set in. Some of the "wits" of the Brigade found a vent to their feelings in composing various prose and poetic effusions on the subject. These were for the most part extremely amusing, and were collected and printed in a mysteriously circulated newspaper called the *Sandhill Lyre*. Copies of this paper were not easily obtainable, however, and only one edition saw the light. I was one of those into whose hands a copy was entrusted. I have it now, and I value it not only for its humorous absurdities but for the sake of the writers.

At Sandhill our camp was close to the village of Longbridge Deverill. Here we lived through a prolonged battle with the mud. The huts for officers and men were sufficiently comfortable, but to get to one's abode was the difficulty; however, as time went on, duckboards were laid down and roads were made, and the approach became a less exhausting labour. The health of the Brigade in spite of the wet remained good. While at Sandhill Camp the supply of Lewis guns was increased from the modest number of two per Battalion to, I think, one per company. The officer selected as Brigade Machine Officer, and who had general charge of the machine gun training of the Brigade,

ON SALISBURY PLAIN, 1915.　　　[To face p. 24.
1. Trench digging.
2. Machine Gunners, 3rd Batt. T.S.
3. Outside the Hutments.

AT LONGBRIDGE DEVERILL

was Captain J. W. E. Murray, of the 2nd Battalion, and he was a welcome addition to the Brigade Mess. At a considerably later date in France the number of Lewis guns per Battalion throughout the Army was gradually brought up to sixteen per Battalion, viz., one to each platoon. A separate unit, the Brigade machine gun company, was also instituted, armed with sixteen Vicker's guns. But that is anticipating events. Longbridge Deverill is memorable principally to me as a time of wet and mud—what we didn't know about mud wasn't worth knowing. Divisional and Brigade exercises took place weekly, wet or fine, and many a sham engagement was fought on the well-known hills round about. On one occasion the G.O.C. in C. Salisbury Plain, ordered that the Tyneside Scottish Brigade, representing a Division, should defend a certain tract of country against an Army Corps represented by the 32nd Division.

Fortune decreed a victory for us, and the G.O.C. in C., who was present watching the operations, at the "Pow-Wow" which followed was good enough to make some very flattering remarks about the work of the Brigade. One point on which he laid particular stress was the quick grasp displayed by company and platoon commanders of the continually changing requirements of the situation, and the resource which they showed in seizing opportunities as they occurred. The smartness of the signallers also attracted his special attention, and the Brigade marched home in great good humour. The officers and men had throughout the long course of arduous training which they had gone through worked with a will, and thoroughly deserved the praises the G.O.C. in C. gave them.

It was very unfortunate that about this time we were to lose the services of two very valuable officers. One of these was Major J. F. MacKay, V.C., the second in command of the 2nd Battalion, who met with a serious accident which laid him up for some considerable time, and prevented his accompanying his Battalion to France. Colonel C. H. Innes Hopkins, commanding the 1st Battalion, who was the other, was unfortunately attacked by influenza, and the doctors absolutely refused to allow him to rejoin his Battalion. Colonel Innes Hopkins was one of the originators of the Tyneside Scottish, and was selected to command the 1st Battalion at the time when it was supposed that owing to the very large numbers of men given by the Tyne to the Northumberland Fusiliers and Durham Light Infantry (Regulars, New Army, and Territorials) it would not be possible to raise more than one Battalion of Tyneside Scottish. It was very largely due to him that the movement met with such great success, and his detachment from his Battalion at this moment was not only an extreme disappointment to him personally, but was felt to be a serious loss to the Brigade. We were all glad to hear at a later date that Colonel Innes Hopkins was eventually given the command of another Battalion which did excellent service in France. It is a matter of common knowledge that Colonel Innes Hopkins suffered the loss of his two sons, both of whom were killed in action.

The officer appointed to succeed to the command of the 1st Battalion was Major C. C. A. Sillery, late Indian Army, a most excellent capable officer who fully maintained the efficiency of his Battalion, and, alas, was killed at the head of it on 1st July, 1916. There had also been a change in the command of the 4th Battalion, Major E. K. Purnell having, to my great regret and to his disgust, been invalided by a medical board. He was replaced by Major W. Lyle of the reserve of officers, who also fell while gallantly leading his Battalion at La Boisselle. At the time when Major Purnell was appointed to the command the condition of this Battalion was not altogether satisfactory, and it was due to his exertions, assisted by his very able adjutant, Captain Mackintosh, that a very high standard of proficiency was reached. It was there-

Lt.-Colonel W. Lyle and Officers,
4th Batt. Tyneside Scottish, 1915.

AT LONGBRIDGE DEVERILL 27

fore a very great disappointment that he should, after all, be unable to take his Battalion to France. One of the events which one remembers most vividly about this time was an extremely unpleasant weather experience. An attack was to be carried out by the Division for the benefit of a party of Japanese officers who were coming down to see it. The Brigade had been kept busy for some days digging a series of trenches on a piece of low-lying ground not far from Sutton Veny, and on the night previous to the attack the weather, which had been fairly fine, changed and the rain came down, a regular continuous deluge, the whole country round becoming a quagmire. It was expected that under such conditions some modifications in the arrangements would be made, but to the surprise of all ranks the original programme was adhered to. For hours before the attack was timed to take place, lying out in the pouring rain officers and men were soaked to the skin. When the astonished Japanese arrived on the scene, they expressed themselves amazed as well they might be at the hardihood of the British troops.

The drenched and dripping companies having wallowed for several hours in the soaked ground, each man became a moving mass of mud from head to toe. Though the language used at the time was regrettably strong, it was, however, satisfactory to be afterwards informed that the Division had gained great kudos by its distinctly amphibian performance, which had unmistakably impressed our Japanese friends. We were much disturbed one day to hear that General Williams had come to serious grief in a motor-car accident. Fortunately it turned out that though he had had a narrow escape and was considerably hurt he would not be incapacitated as was at first feared. He had, however, to lay up much against his will for some considerable time. It was announced on one occasion that the Division was to be reviewed on a certain date by his Majesty the King. Though all ranks were by this time sufficiently trained so far as field work was concerned, little time had been given to ceremonial drill, so that some polishing-up was necessary, and we got so far as to have a rehearsal of the whole Division on a suitable piece of ground some eight to ten miles away. The rehearsal went off very satisfactorily, but the review by his Majesty did not materialise.

I think it was early in December that we were informed that we were to be held in readiness to proceed at short notice to Egypt. Though the majority of us would, I believe, have preferred to go to France, the main battle theatre, still we were all delighted to think that we were really going at last to get a move on. Sun helmets were issued to the Brigade, officers provided themselves with thin clothing suitable to a hotter climate, and we were ready to move when the order was suddenly cancelled. The move was " off." The helmets were returned to store, and things were " as you were." All ranks were bitterly disappointed; many of the officers and men had been training for well over a year, and had had the mortification of seeing friends and acquaintances with half their experience shipped off to France. It seemed as if the 34th Division would never get away. Representatives of the Tyneside Scottish Committee, who had arranged to visit us prior to our move, came down about this time from Newcastle, and were accommodated in the various Battalion camps. We had a dinner in honour of the occasion in the Brigade Headquarters Mess, and among those present were Lord Armstrong, Mr Alex. Wilkie, M.P., Colonel Sir Thomas Oliver, Colonel Johnstone Wallace, Colonel Joseph Reed, and Mr J. R. Hall. The next day being Sunday some of these gentlemen attended the Brigade Church of England service. After the service a speech to the Brigade was made by Colonel Sir Thomas Oliver, as chairman of the Tyneside Scottish Committee, and he was invited to take the salute at the subsequent march past.

CHAPTER IV

DEPARTURE FOR FRANCE

IN spite of the fact that very drastic weeding out of " crocks " had from time to time taken place, the Brigade was well above its full establishment, and the physique was excellent. A bombing competition, open to teams from each Infantry unit in the Division, took place at Sutton Veny just before Christmas, 1915. The first prize, given by General Ingouville-Williams, was carried off by the team sent in by 2nd Battalion Tyneside Scottish. When at Alnwick a team of the 2nd Battalion had previously much distinguished itself by winning the important Cross Country Competition held at York in the summer, open to all units in the Northern Command, so that we had every reason to be satisfied with the prowess of the Brigade in the sporting line. The appointment of officers prior to the formation of the Brigade had been in the hands of the Committee, who, however, usually acted on the advice of the commanding officers. After the Brigade was formed and until the War Office took it over the appointments were left to me subject to War Office approval, and I made it a rule to consider no application unless the applicant could show either previous military experience or had served in the O.T.C. or in the ranks. The number of candidates for commissions was large, the majority being entirely ignorant of the duties they would have to perform, and were obviously unsuited to act as instructors and platoon commanders. I always encouraged them to enlist and apply again for a commission in a few months' time.

On one occasion a young man presented himself at Brigade Headquarters at Alnwick, and said that he had come up from London with a view to obtaining a commission in the Tyneside Scottish. His testimonials were excellent, and from his build, general appearance, and manner one judged his age to be about nineteen or twenty. He had had previous experience in a Public School O.T.C., and he would have been accepted had I not noticed to my surprise that the official application form signed by his father showed his age to be a little over sixteen, which the boy at once admitted to be correct. In view of the War Office orders that no one under the age of nineteen was to be appointed, I had regretfully to inform the youth that under the circumstances he could not be accepted. A few days later he again arrived from London with a new form made out, on which the date of his birth as given by his father showed his age to be now nineteen. I thereupon accepted him, and appointed him to one of the Battalions. He soon proved a most useful young officer, and later gained the Military Cross for his work in the field. I fear the moral of this story is obscure.

While we were at Sandhill Camp a signalling section of the R.E. was attached to the Brigade, and later accompanied it to France. The section was under the command of Temporary Second-Lieutenant Dowse, who was later to prove his worth on very many occasions in the trenches. After a gallant and eventful career he was very severely wounded in France, but just lived to get home. His father wrote to me that his last words were that " He had always tried to do his duty." He had indeed done so with admirable success. Always cheery and enthusiastic in his work, no task, however unpleasant, was too much for him. His section worked splendidly for him, and it was with profound and sincere regret that we in the Brigade Mess heard that he had succumbed to his wounds. I have always looked upon the high

Lieut.-Colonel A. P. A. Elphinstone and Officers, 3rd. Batt. Tyneside Scottish, 1915.

DEPARTURE FOR FRANCE

state of efficiency reached by the Brigade as in a large measure due to the efforts of my friend, our Brigade Major, Major T. Soutry. His common sense and unfailing tact resulted in the relations of the Brigade office to the various units being particularly cordial, which is not always the case. Many a time I found his sound judgment of the greatest possible value, and when he subsequently left us on promotion to a higher staff appointment he left a gap which was hard to fill.

The only one of the original commanding officers of the Brigade who at this stage remained with us and accompanied his Battalion to France was Lieutenant-Colonel A. P. A. Elphinstone, commanding the 3rd Battalion, a man whose sterling good qualities made him beloved by every officer and man in his Battalion. He was, moreover, a first-class commanding officer. He died as he would have chosen, at the head of his men, but I can never think of those days at Alnwick and Sutton Veny without recalling him as he then was, no longer young but full of vigour and good spirits, fearing nothing except that his age might possibly prevent his sailing with his men to France. But, to push on with the story. Towards the latter half of December it was rumoured, to the general satisfaction, on apparently good authority that the Division was to sail before Christmas for France, but as the days passed and no orders on the subject were received, the pessimists prophesied that it was a case of Egypt over again. Suddenly, early in January, 1916, it was announced that the Division had received definite orders to move at once to France, and detailed plans for the move of the Infantry Brigades and other units were issued.

One Battalion of the Tyneside Scottish was to proceed *via* Folkestone and Boulogne, and the Brigade Headquarters and the remainder of the Brigade *via* Southampton and Havre. The 4th Battalion, under Lieutenant-Colonel Lyle, was accordingly detailed to move *via* Folkestone. Both officers and men had been for so long expecting orders to move, and had all made their necessary arrangements, that the final packing up and departure of each Battalion was carried out very quietly, and without any sort of a hitch. The entraining of the transport animals and wagons was particularly well done by the regimental transport officers, under the supervision of Lieutenant Ker. Some of the wives and families of the married officers were living temporarily in or near Longbridge Deverill, and their farewells, too many, alas, final, were made in the privacy of home. All officers and men who had hitherto been serving with the Brigade who were in excess of establishment had, much to their annoyance, been sent to the depot of the Northumberland Fusiliers at Newcastle. As orderly officers to Brigadiers were not allowed for in the establishment, I had very reluctantly to part with Lieutenant Turnbull, who returned to the 1st Battalion in the capacity of platoon commander. He had been the greatest help to me since the early days of the Brigade, and I was extremely sorry to lose him. He was afterwards wounded while commanding his platoon at La Boisselle, and subsequently served with distinction as a Major in another unit in Italy. All ranks breathed a sigh of relief, we were really off to France at last. The move was quite uneventful. The trip across Channel was done during the night of 6th January, 1916. On arriving at Havre I found that the Brigade, which was being temporarily accommodated in rest camps in or near the town, was to move the next day by rail. Our destination was kept a secret, and it was not until we arrived at St Omer and were told to detrain there that we knew that we had come to the end of our train journey. The time taken from Havre to St Omer *via* Calais was fourteen hours.

CHAPTER V

A VISIT TO THE FRONT LINE TRENCHES

THE British Commander-in-Chief's Headquarters were at this time at St Omer, but there were no troops other than details which formed part of the headquarters actually quartered in the town. The 34th Division which was to form part of the G.H.Q. reserve was to be billeted in various villages a few miles east of St Omer. The Tyneside Scottish Brigade took up its quarters in a number of houses scattered over three villages, with the Brigade Headquarters at the Château Cartieux in the village of Wardreques. Here we remained for about a week, and the officers and men began their acquaintance with French village life. We were, roughly speaking, about thirty miles from the firing line, and it was only occasionally that the sound of guns became audible, but all ranks now were exhilarated by the feeling that the time of preliminaries was nearly over, and that the result of our many months of arduous training would soon be put to the test in real earnest. While we were here route marching was practised daily, and the transport and equipment generally were carefully inspected. After the mud of Salisbury Plain the work seemed very light, and the men had a comparatively easy time.

One day we were informed that the C.-in-C., Field-Marshal Sir Douglas Haig, and Marshal Joffre would review the Division the following day, and arrangements were made accordingly. The Tyneside Scottish Brigade was to be drawn up in line along the main road to St Omer, and took up its position in good time. The time given for the inspection was 12 noon. It was a very cold day with a biting wind and sleet. It was not until 3 o'clock that the group of motor-cars containing the two C's.-in-C. and their staff were seen approaching. The men who had been allowed to fall out and stamp about to keep warm were hastily fallen in, and by the time the first car, occupied by Sir Douglas Haig and Marshal Joffre, reached the right of our line the companies were smartly " dressed." The various Battalions presented arms as the car reached them. Marshal Joffre sat on the right, and as the car passed slowly along the line it was evident from his expression that the French C.-in-C. was very well satisfied with the appearance of the newly landed reinforcements. Later on we received word officially that Marshal Joffre was extremely pleased with the soldierly appearance of the men.

At the Château Cartieux the Brigade Headquarters was in clover. The owner of the house and his wife, well-to-do people (he was the head of a local paper factory), lived on the premises, and did everything possible to make us comfortable. My bedroom was a spacious apartment, extremely well furnished, and in addition to good bedrooms for the staff there was a dining-room set apart for us as a Brigade Mess. Madame herself superintended the cooking, which was excellent, and the few days we spent there is a very pleasant recollection which it is difficult to reconcile with the usually accepted conditions of a theatre of war, so far at least as humble Brigadiers are concerned. It was while we were here that we had the pleasure of a visit from the Duke of Northumberland, who was accompanied by Captain A. D. M. Napier of the Northumbrian Territorial Association. The Duke was engaged in visiting the various units of the Northumberland Fusiliers of which he was Honorary-Colonel, and we arranged a luncheon party in his honour to which

BRIGADE HD. QR. STAFF, TYNESIDE SCOTTISH, 1915.

[*To face page* 34.

THE FRONT LINE TRENCHES 35

the commanding officers of the Battalions of the Brigade were invited. In spite of somewhat short notice our hostess managed to produce a luncheon of extra special quality, and our host unearthed some bottles of " grand vin " to mark the occasion.

In order to show their friends and relations at home that they were now really at last in the war zone some of the more imaginative of the men when writing home evidently thought the local war colour should be laid on thick, and though we were still far from the sight and hardly within sound of the guns, the most graphic descriptions were given of " shells which, as I write, are bursting all round me," and other details of the dangers and horrors in which the writer lived.

As a matter of fact nothing could have exceeded the peace and quiet of these few days near St Omer—not even a bomb fell. The company officers who acted as censors naturally derived a considerable amount of amusement from these effusions, and though, of course, no names were mentioned, one often heard and thoroughly enjoyed the tales of hairbreadth escapes which were so vividly described but had never actually occurred. Though the censor's work was irksome it was, therefore, not devoid of humour; on the contrary some of the letter-writers were a constant source of joy to the weary censor; for instance, there was the man, who we will call Private Johnstone, who wrote weekly to his wife in a very dignified tone, always beginning his letters " Dear Mrs Johnstone," and signing himself " Yours truly, Mr Johnstone."

There was close to the Château Cartieux a large pottery factory, and Captain Marr, the Staff Captain, was fortunate enough to be able to arrange with the owner that a big tank which was usually full of hot water which ran in on one side and out at the other, should be utilised as a bath by the men. The charge was a penny a head. The tank held about a dozen men at a time, so that in a few days the whole Brigade was able to get a bath, and the owner made a good thing out of it. In later days the bath system behind the lines was very well organised. Every man on coming out of the trenches at the end of his spell there, was marched to the baths where he was also given a complete change of clothing in place of his wet and muddy ones, but at the time I am writing of we had not arrived at such a civilised condition.

At this period the Divisional Headquarters were at a château about two miles from Château Cartieux. General Williams often came to see the Brigade, and there were occasional conferences of Brigadiers and the Divisional Staff at Divisional Headquarters. General Sir Herbert Plumer, who was commanding the 2nd Army, had his headquarters at Cassel; and Brigadier-General Fitton, C.B., A.D.C., who was commanding the 101st Infantry Brigade, and I arranged one day to motor over and pay our respects. We were fortunate enough to find the General free.

The headquarters offices were in a large building on the top of the conical hill on which Cassel is built. We had both previously served under General Plumer, and he very kindly gave us a lot of very useful information, and in the course of conversation suggested that we might like to visit one or two places in his Army area. We were delighted at the chance, and it was arranged that we should motor to Mount Kemmel, where a very good view over the Boche lines was obtainable, and should also spend a night at Ypres. The visit to Mount Kemmel passed off without incident, and I think it was the next day that General Fitton and I set off in a Divisional car for Ypres. We had been furnished with the necessary papers by the 2nd Army Authorities, and it had been arranged that General Fitton was to visit the 15th Brigade, which early in the war had been commanded by General Ingouville-Williams, and was now under the command of Brigadier-General

THE FRONT LINE TRENCHES 37

C. Nicholson, and that I was to visit the 16th Brigade which was commanded by Brigadier-General Bridgeford who was formerly in my own Regiment—the Manchesters.

The two Brigades formed part of the 6th Division and were at the time holding two adjacent sectors of the trenches on the canal bank at Ypres. We travelled *via* Popperinghe and reported ourselves to the G.O.C. 6th Division, whose headquarters were established in a magnificent château a few miles west of Ypres. The G.O.C. 6th Division explained to us the best way of reaching the Brigades, and gave us an excellent lunch. The Huns seemed to be unusually quiet though a certain number of shells were bursting in Ypres. The bit of the road between Popperinghe and Ypres was, however, much cut up by the enemy fire, and we were told that every now and then the Huns made movement along it difficult. After lunch we went on by car to Ypres and motored through the town, passing close to the ruins of the Cathedral and the Cloth Hall. The whole place was a melancholy ruin, silent and empty. Occasionally a shell would burst and a column of dust would rise from the debris of a demolished house. There was no sign of life except for a stray soldier hurriedly making his way along a deserted street or what had been a street. On arriving at a certain corner we were met and told that the car could proceed no further as it then would come under the direct observation of the Hun, and so from there we walked to the canal not very far away.

I remember that we were amused at the extreme rapidity with which the car disappeared in the direction we had come. Ypres certainly was not a place to linger in. In a few minutes we reached the headquarters of the 15th Brigade and met Brigadier-General Nicholson, who was later to succeed General Ingouville-Williams in the command of the 34th Division. These headquarters were excavated in the high canal bank on the side away from the canal. After a short talk I left Brigadier-General Fitton at these headquarters and went off with an orderly as guide to the headquarters of the 16th Brigade. Before leaving General Fitton we arranged that I should meet him at the 15th Brigade Headquarters the next day at 12 noon, and motor back with him to our Division. I found the 16th Brigade Headquarters were upon the opposite side of the canal a short distance away. The canal is about sixty yards broad, and the two banks were connected by a number of light narrow foot-bridges, by one of which we crossed. The 16th Brigade Headquarters was installed in a series of dug-outs cut in the canal bank, on the side of the bank nearest the canal. The top of the bank was about ten to twelve feet above the water-level. Between the bank and the canal was a narrow extemporary footpath giving access to the dug-outs. A few of the dug-outs were made of iron sheeting covered with earth, but the majority were merely excavations in the side of the bank, each about seven feet square—the walls and roof of timber—with about six feet of earth above. The interior of the dug-outs used as the Brigade offices and quarters for the Brigadier and the staff officers were roughly furnished with a table and a chair or two, evidently picked out of ruined houses in Ypres.

General Bridgeford's Brigade was holding a bit of the line, his front trenches being about two miles from the canal, and it was arranged that he would accompany me early the following morning to his front line trenches and generally show me round. I was given a just completed iron-framed dug-out to sleep in, and turned in early after dinner. Next day before sunrise we made a start for the trenches, and beyond the struggles with the mud our visit was uneventful. We visited the front line, but beyond an occasional shell fired by the Boche, apparently at nothing in particular, and

THE FRONT LINE TRENCHES 39

a few rifle shots at intervals, all was quiet. A certain number of shells passed overhead on their way to Ypres, and our guns maintained a slow fire. The weather was very dull, and the view of the flat country was distinctly uninteresting. One, however, got a first impression of existence in the trenches, and gathered much useful information for future guidance. Though this happened to be a quiet day, there were many occasions when matters were very different, and the Ypres salient was often subjected to a murderous bombardment, and was about the " unhealthiest " part of the line. The previous evening the enemy had suddenly opened a very heavy fire which lasted a few minutes only on some transport which had after dark brought up supplies to a dump in the town. We could hear the wagons rattling off over the cobblestones as they hastily made off. This was a game which both sides played sometimes with considerable success.

CHAPTER VI

AN UNOFFICIAL INSPECTION

WE returned to the canal about 10 o'clock, and shortly afterwards received a message telling us that General Fitton had been wounded during the night. It seemed that he had accompanied the G.O.C. 15th Brigade up to the front trenches, and while there had been hit by a rifle bullet. He was said to be suffering from a flesh wound in the leg, and had been taken to hospital. I therefore had to make the return journey by myself, calling again at the Divisional Headquarters at Château Flaminghe on my way. It was a shock to us all who knew him well to hear a day or two afterwards that General Fitton had died from his wounds. He was the first casualty suffered by the 34th Division. A very distinguished and able soldier, he would, no doubt, had he lived have risen to high rank, and his untimely death was a distinct loss to the Division as well as to his own Brigade.

He was succeeded in the command of the 101st Infantry Brigade by Brigadier-General R. C. Gore, C.M.G., A. and S. Highlanders. The command of the 103rd (Tyneside Irish) Brigade had been held for more or less short periods by various officers, but shortly before the Division left England the command of the Brigade had been given to Brigadier-General N. G. Cameron—who had been until then senior general staff officer on the Divisional Staff, so that after General Fitton's death the three Infantry Brigades were commanded by Brigadier-General Gore, 101st, myself, 102nd, and Brigadier-General Cameron, 103rd.

AN UNOFFICIAL INSPECTION 41

It was arranged that the various units of our Division should each be temporarily attached for instructional purposes to a similar unit of a Division which was holding a section of the trenches in order to get the necessary experience of trench life prior to actually taking over a portion of the line. The 102nd Tyneside Scottish Brigade was accordingly ordered to move to Steenbecque, a place much nearer the front line. From there units would be sent up to be attached to a corresponding unit in the trenches. We of the Brigade Headquarters made our adieux to Monsieur and Madame with very cordial feelings on both sides, and the Brigade marched to Steenbecque, where it arrived on the 25th January, 1916. The 1st Battalion was billeted in the town, the 2nd, 3rd, and 4th Battalions in hutments and tents close by. While we were here the Brigade was inspected by Lieutenant-General Sir William Pulteney, commanding the 3rd Corps of which the Division was to form part. The Brigade was formed up in the largest grass field available, and after the inspection the Corps Commander addressed the men, and expressed himself as much pleased with their soldierly appearance, and with their extreme steadiness on parade. A few days later it was announced that Lord Kitchener would inspect part of the Division on parade, but that as his time was limited the inspection of the Infantry would be confined to the 101st Infantry Brigade. That Brigade therefore was paraded, but as I had known Lord Kitchener for many years, having served in the Egyptian Army and in South Africa under him, I was anxious that the Tyneside Scottish Brigade should also have the honour of being inspected by the great Field-Marshal. I therefore obtained permission for the Brigade to line the road by which he would approach on his way to see the 101st Brigade. When his car came up to the right of my line I ventured to stop it, and opening the door asked him if he would like to see a fine Brigade though it was not on the programme. Lord Kitchener at once agreed, got out, walked along the entire front, and was received with vociferous cheers by each Company as he passed. He was in the best of spirits, laughing and talking, and said he was delighted with the look of the men. All ranks were very glad of the chance of seeing him at close quarters.

During this unauthorised inspection, however, the Corps and the Divisional Commanders were with the 101st Infantry Brigade awaiting Lord Kitchener's arrival, who seemed to be unaccountably late, and I was told later, privately, that remarks were made which would lead one to suppose that I was temporarily in considerable disfavour, which was perhaps not altogether surprising. This was to prove the last time that I was to see Lord Kitchener. When he died I was one of many insignificant soldiers who lost a good friend.

It was during the time that the Brigade was at Steenbecque that I and the Brigade Staff were attached for instructional purposes for a week to a Brigade of the 8th Division which was holding the line east of Fleurbaix, a few miles south of Armentieres. Major Soutry, Captain Marrs, Lieutenant Dowse (signalling officer), and myself motored to Fleurbaix and found a Brigade Headquarters established in a ramshackle farmhouse on a road about one and a half miles from the front trench. Here we were all carefully coached by the Brigadier and his staff in the art of trench warfare and routine work, particularly as regarded the piece of the line which the Brigade was holding. We visited the trenches daily, and gradually the intricacies of the various lines and " strong points " became clear. We studied the methods of relief, system of supply, and the numerous other matters particularly connected with trench life, and at the end of the week we each of us had become fully conversant with our

AN UNOFFICIAL INSPECTION 43

respective duties. By this time the platoons, companies, and eventually Battalions had all been through the mill attached to Battalions and Brigades in the 8th Division for the purpose, and both officers and men had become used to the peculiar conditions of trench life. We had had a few casualties, our first, and it was no longer necessary for men to invent incidents.

When writing home shells actually did " burst around me as I write," and men did die suddenly near-by. It was all quite real. The Brigade was now " bloodied " and ready to take its place in the arena. Our period of tuition being now over the Brigade was detailed to take over the piece of the line held by a Brigade of the 8th Division, and accordingly we were ordered to move by route march from Steenbecque, where we had once more been temporarily concentrated, to Fleurbaix *via* La Motte, Neuf Berquin and Estaires. We marched out of Steenbecque on the 27th and reached Estaires on the 29th January, 1916. The men marched well, and the number who fell out owing to sore feet was commendably few. It was interesting when passing through La Motte Forest to see the stacks of timber cut up into suitable lengths for use in the construction of trenches lying along the sides of the road. This forest is State property and must have been of immense value for local war requirements. There were a certain number of wild pheasants and other game in the forest, and it was rumoured that occasionally the Corps Commander and his staff who were quartered in the château on the estate were able to take some well-earned relaxation in the shape of a little shooting. It was also said that when the French local authorities sent in an account for £250, as a season's rent for the shoot, it was considered as . . . well, that the sport was hardly worth the money.

The country is, of course, in this neighbourhood very flat and uninteresting, and the roads are bordered by deep ditches usually full of water. During a ten minutes' halt one day Major Soutry's horse, a very fine animal, distinguished itself by sliding off the road into the ditch, and was very nearly drowned. Major Soutry did eventually succeed in getting the animal out alive, but the saddle and the gear attached to it were in a bad way. I am afraid the language used on this occasion was quite up to any previous Flanders standard. Major-General Ingouville-Williar s, the Divisional Commander, used frequently to appear at unexpected corners, having often ridden across country to have a look at the various Brigades on the march. He usually remarked to the commanding officers on the excellent turn out of their Battalions, and it was seldom that he had any fault to find. The Battalions marched well, and with the pipers at their head went by with a swing. The pipers were a particular source of joy to the youthful inhabitants of the villages.

There was an intense feeling of esprit de corps in each unit and throughout the Brigade at that time, which was only partially destroyed after the July battle, when so many of the original volunteers were killed or wounded and so lost to the Brigade, and who were replaced by officers and men of other units with no Tyneside associations. Officers and men were in excellent fettle, and marched along fully alive to the fact that they had a hard time before them, but quite determined as they always were that they would show that the Tyneside Scottish were more than a match for any Boche Brigade, and that victory in the long run would be theirs. I never had a doubt on the subject and was never in the future to have cause to think that I had in the slightest degree over-estimated the great fighting qualities of the old Brigade.

On arrival at Estaires, which was about six miles behind the lines, the Battalions were billeted in the houses along each side of the long main street of

PIPERS, 3RD. BATT. TYNESIDE SCOTTISH, 1915.

AN UNOFFICIAL INSPECTION 45

the town. The Brigade Headquarters was established in a large and somewhat pretentious modern house with well-furnished rooms. The bedrooms were particularly luxurious, and the dining-room boasted of an ingle-nook in which was a roaring wood fire, most welcome as the weather was very cold. Here we had a conference of our Brigade Staff, and that of the Brigade that we were to relieve, which was attended by the C.O.'s of our Brigade, and we worked out the details for the relief that was to take place after dark on the following day. Advance parties from each Battalion were to be sent forward to get a knowledge of the trenches, and to take over the trench stores, etc., etc., and arrange the local details as to the reliefs; guides were arranged to meet the incoming units at certain selected spots and lead them to their own particular bit of the trench. The Battalion Quartermasters and Transport officers had to be given exact instructions to prevent any possible hitch occurring, but at length everything had been fully discussed and everyone concerned knew what he had to do.

At the house we occupied as the Brigade Headquarters there had been left a man and his wife who acted as caretakers. The owner was away. The wife we found to be an excellent cook, so we enjoyed meals which differed very considerably from our usual repasts. Colonel Elphinstone, I think it was, who discovered that very fair champagne at extremely moderate prices was to be obtained at a shop in the town, while at another shop *pâté de foie gras* was being sold by the pound. Very excellent it was and comparatively cheap. That night our dinner party was quite a festive affair. Colonel Elphinstone came to dinner, and also Colonel Sillery, both of whom were always amusing and good company, and we had a very cheery evening. The caretaker informed us with bated breath that the house some time before had been honoured for a night by no less a personage than King George, and that his Majesty had occupied the room I had. The room certainly was not unworthy of a Prince. On more frequent occasions one found the accommodation anything but princely—quite the other way—but war does produce strange mixtures of luxury and squalor. I recollect in Egypt in 1882, when my Regiment was quartered in the Harem apartments of the Khedive's Palace at Alexandria (it is perhaps unnecessary to say that the ladies had all been removed elsewhere), the Captains of companies occupied a luxurious *salon*, with marble walls, silk hangings and satin divans, while the subalterns inhabited an adjacent scullery. My blankets were laid out in the sink which, in the opinion of my soldier servant, was for various reasons preferable to the floor, and he was right. However, this is getting a long way from the Tyneside Scottish.

CHAPTER VII

THE BRIGADE TAKES OVER A PORTION OF THE LINE

OUR move had to be timed so that the head of the column should arrive at a certain point on the road about four miles from Estaires at dusk. At this point the guides supplied by the Brigade met their respective units, and led them to their destinations. As the troops got nearer to the enemy, the size of each party diminished in order to offer as small a target as possible should the enemy open fire on them. The relief was accomplished without any particular incidents, and the Tyneside Scottish for the first time was holding the line as a Brigade. The Brigade Headquarters was established in the same small farmhouse at Fleurbaix as we had previously occupied while we were undergoing our course of instruction, and when the reports had all come in by telephone from the various units that each portion of the line had been duly taken over, the Brigadier and his staff of the outgoing Brigade, with a sigh of relief, said " Good-bye," got into a car, and disappeared into the darkness. The Brigade was now for a week or ten days attached to the 8th Division, during which time units of that Division were relieved by the 34th Division, and at the expiration of that time Major-General Ingouville-Williams took over the command of that portion of the line, and the 34th Division became one of the fighting Divisions in France.

While we were attached to the 8th Division we were treated with great consideration, and everything possible was done to help us, and all in an extremely tactful way. Being still new to the game, many little points cropped up from time to time which required attention, things which in course of time became second nature. All such matters were adjusted all the more readily owing to the tact of the 8th Division staff, whose work struck us as not only excellent, but entirely frictionless. Perhaps as " Tenderfeet " we were let down easily, but whatever the reason was we all felt that we were under a most considerate as well as capable staff. After we had been in the line a few days, we were very pleased to hear that we were to have a visit from some of the members of the Committee, and arrangements were accordingly made. The accommodation of the farmhouse was not exactly luxurious. The farm buildings formed the usual hollow square, one side of which, that which faced the road, was the living house. This house consisted of one room with a wooden partition shutting off one end in which was a bedstead and a loft above. The interior of the square was taken up with the inevitable dung pit of these parts with a raised brick path running round it opening on to the stables, cow-houses, pigsties, etc.; it was not an ideal dwelling by any means. The living-room we used as the Brigade Mess Room, and by right of being the senior officer I occupied the partitioned enclosure as a bedroom. The staff slept some in an adjacent cottage and some in the loft. The house was fairly intact, having been hardly touched by shells. The Battalion commanders were using as their headquarters the remains of what had been farm buildings or cottages much nearer the front line; the Battalion Headquarters of the two Battalions in support being a little further back than the other two.

The custom was for the Brigadier to pay a visit of inspection to some part of the line daily, and to call at one or more of the Battalion Headquarters *en route*. The first time I went to see Colonel

A PORTION OF THE LINE

Elphinstone I found him and his adjutant in a very ramshackle remnant of a small house. The greater part of the upper walls and all the floors of the rooms above had been blown away, but in some mysterious way the roof remained almost intact, so that the ground floor room had an unusually lofty appearance. It was raining hard at the time, and the water poured into the room through the large gaps in the wall, and the roof leaked badly. At the time of my arrival water seemed to be dripping from everywhere, and the stone floor was a puddle, but that did not seem to in any way affect Elphinstone, who was just as bright and cheery as ever, and was loud in praises of his " house," and his luck in getting such good quarters. I remember suggesting to him that after the war he might arrange to buy the place! Colonel Lyle had his headquarters at this time in a particularly warm spot. It was on a road which seemed to attract the frequent attention of the Boches. When I first went to see him somebody in the Boche lines had evidently taken it into his head to strafe Lyle's Headquarters, and things were lively for a few minutes. Lyle was a remarkably good-natured fellow, but somewhat hot-tempered, and I arrived just in time to hear him telling an N.C.O. of the sappers who had, contrary to orders, apparently marched a small party of men along the road behind Lyle's abode and so attracted the enemy's fire, exactly what he thought of him. The language was free and suited to the occasion, and no doubt impressed the delinquent with the enormity of his offence. However, when the straffing was over it was found that no casualties had occurred and little damage done. Lyle was full of common sense, and though he was not one of the original Tyneside Scots he very soon fell into the Brigade groove, and became as keen as any of us to maintain esprit de corps in every possible way. He was always intensely proud of his Battalion and its doings, and he had reason to be. Sillery's Headquarters were in what had been a public house, and he was comparatively comfortable. I cannot now recall the whereabouts of Colonel Dunbar Stuart's billet at this time. After each Battalion had been in the front trenches for a spell, usually of five days, it was withdrawn and relieved by a Battalion in support, and the necessary exchanges of Battalion and Company Headquarters took place. The Brigades at this period were usually relieved by a Brigade in Divisional Reserve after about sixteen days in the line, but this entirely depended upon circumstances. Later on, at Armentieres, our Brigade held the line for one spell of over three months.

The Company Headquarters were as a rule in so-called dugouts, but in this part of the line the cover obtained was not really adequate, as, owing to the fact that water was dug into at a depth of about two or three feet, no dugouts could be made. The cover for the men in the front trenches was merely lean-to's put up against the parapet, with a few rows of sand bags as head cover. This was good enough for rifle and machine gun fire or even whizz-bangs, but was useless against any heavier shells or the projectiles thrown by trench mortars. It was a pleasure when going round the trenches to see and talk to the men, who were always cheery and amusing. They were delighted to be in France, and looked upon the whole thing as a big joke. There was, however, no slackness so far as duty was concerned, and the discipline was admirable, as in fact it always was. I used to frequently visit and discuss rations with the cooks, but the men seldom had any complaints to make. I soon found that the cheese ration was much in excess of the requirements; about half the ration was not eaten so far as my Brigade was concerned, and at a later date I officially suggested that half the cheese ration would suffice. The correspondence, however, when it returned to me, showed that the opinion of the medical authorities was against any reduction. Cheese, it was stated, contained a large amount of " calories." It was not worth while in my humble position to pursue the question, but it seems to me that uneaten cheese would do no man much good, however many " calories " it contained, and the waste of large quantities of cheese would be avoided if a lesser amount were issued. Some Brigades, no doubt, ate all their cheese; others did not. It depended upon the habits of the men and the part of the country they came from.

I am afraid that while we were at Fleurbaix, we as a Brigade were for a short time by no means blessed by the troops in our neighbourhood, especially those in Divisional Reserve; in fact the language used was, I was told, both loud and expressive. What happened was this: There was a signal which was only to be used in case of vital urgency, viz., the S.O.S. It consisted of a group of several coloured rockets to be sent up by an officer in the front line if the enemy attacked in serious force, and on no account was to be used for a lesser emergency. One night the enemy attempted a raid, a not unusual occurrence. It failed, and our men drove the raiders off without much difficulty, but alas! owing to some confusion in the wording of a verbal order by a company officer the S.O.S. signal suddenly flared aloft. Instantly the Brigades on our right and left, and our own Battalions in support, got under way to carry out the programme laid down for such an emergency. The signal was repeated to the rear by telephone, the Brigade in Divisional Reserve, snug in billets some miles in rear, was turned out, the heavy artillery came into action, and staff officers were roused from their slumbers to deal with the grave emergency. Major Soutry and I were at the telephone endeavouring to elucidate the report from Commanding Officers, and at last to our horror we found that the whole thing was a false alarm! It was a terrible moment; however

I reported by telephone to the Divisional Headquarters in as unconcerned a manner as I could manage what had occurred. The staff officer who took my message said little, but the following day the chief staff officer happened to call. He had various minor matters to discuss, and incidentally, apparently rather as an after-thought, just mentioned the incident lightly as one which was if possible to be avoided. It was well done, and had exactly the right effect. We never transgressed again in this way.

The members of the Committee who came to see us at Fleurbaix were Sir Thomas Oliver, Colonel Joseph Cowen, Colonel Johnstone Wallace, and Colonel Joseph Reed. They arrived one afternoon in motor-cars and remained with us until the following day. Owing to the want of accommodation in the house it was decided that our guests should occupy two little "Armstrong" canvas huts which the R.E. had put up on piles in the dung pit. Major Soutry and I had previously occupied them during the time we were attached to the Brigade of the 8th Division. To get at them one had to walk along a narrow, slippery plank causeway across the pit. The surroundings were therefore not exactly all that could be desired, but it was the best that we could do. That evening we had a very cheery little dinner, and in view of a projected visit to the front trenches next morning our guests turned in early. It was a dark, wet, and bitterly cold night, and the journey across the pit was a somewhat formidable undertaking, but all went well until one of our guests, who was following the guide, Captain Murray, along the plank, slipped off, and with a yell rolled into the unsavoury depths below, followed by Captain Murray, who clutched tight, had no chance. I had not left the house and was not an eye-witness of the incident, but I gathered the next morning that the spectacle presented when the two unfortunate gentlemen eventually succeeded in extri-

COLONEL JOSEPH REED
Hon. Colonel 2nd Tyneside Scottish
(Trustee Cowen Fund)

COLONEL SIR THOMAS OLIVER
Hon. Colonel 1st Tyneside Scottish
(Chairman Tyneside Scottish Com.)

COLONEL SIR JOHNSTONE WALLACE, K.B.E.
Chairman Tyneside Brigades Committee, and Trustee Cowen Fund.

[*To face p.* 52.

A PORTION OF THE LINE 53

cating themselves was beyond words to describe, though the language used by the gentlemen themselves in the course of their struggles attained a standard which quite adequately described their emotions. The next morning, after an early breakfast, Major Soutry and I personally conducted the party down to the front line. There was a small amount of straffing, just enough to give interest to the visit, and Colonel Reed had the pleasure of losing off a few rounds at the Boches. After a rapid survey of various points of interest, the party returned to Brigade Headquarters. The Committee lunched with us, and then left in motor-cars to visit Armentieres, prior to returning to England. While they were with us the Boches, who frequently dropped shells near our headquarters, managed to hit our roof and a few tiles came off. The Committee could therefore safely say they had been under shell-fire.

One of the points to which great attention had been given by the 8th Divisional Staff was the laying down of light trolley lines by which stores of all kinds could be easily got up at night nearly to the front trenches. The system was well organised, and compared very favourably with similar systems in other parts of the line which we later occupied. There was also never any apparent shortage of duck-boards and other material for trench construction and repair. The trolley system saved much carrying by fatigue parties, and though the Boche tried his best to destroy the lines of rail, he never succeeded while we were there in seriously upsetting the working arrangements, though repairs were frequently necessary daily and nightly. The 34th Division was, however, soon ordered to move to another sector, and we shortly found ourselves holding the line just south of Armentieres. The front trench was about two and a half miles east of Armentieres railway station, the trench line running almost due north and south. The left of our line rested on the

Armentieres-Lille road, where we joined another Division, and just behind our left was the village of Chappelle d'Armentieres, or what remained of it, which straggled on both sides of the road for a considerable distance back almost to the outskirts of Armentieres. The No-Man's-Land between our front trenches and the Boches' front trench varied in this sector from fifty to four hundred yards. The support line was about seventy yards in rear of the front line, and the reserve line was about a thousand yards from the front line. About another thousand yards behind the reserve line were the positions of the batteries of the Divisional Artillery, usually posted in sheltered spots, mostly in houses or under artificial cover in order to escape observation by enemy aeroplanes. The Brigade Headquarters was in a house in a street on the outskirts of Armentieres, connected by telephone with the Divisional Headquarters and with the office of the officer commanding the Artillery of the Brigade area and with the headquarters of each of the Battalions of the Brigade. The length of our Brigade front was about one thousand two hundred yards, and on our right we joined the 101st Brigade. The 103rd Brigade was in reserve in the village of Erquinghem, some little way in rear of the 101st Brigade. The Divisional Headquarters was at Croire de Bac, a village about four miles south-west of Armentieres, and the transport was collected by Brigades in various centres not far from Divisional Headquarters. The R.E. yard was in the village of Erquinghem. The country on our side of No-Man's-Land was very flat, but behind the Boche lines the ground rose and formed the Aubers Ridge, behind which, out of sight from our side, is the city of Lille. The Armentieres-Lille road crossed No-Man's-Land, and just inside the Boche lines was the village of Wez Macquart which was built along each side of the road, so that while Chappelle d'Armentieres was along the road in our lines, the village of

Maj.-Gen. Sir C. L. Nicholson, K.C.B., C.M.G.
(Commanding 34th Division, 1916-17-18).

Brig.-Gen. Trevor Ternan, C.B., C.M.G., D.S.O.

Major-General Edward Charles Ingouville-Williams, C.B.
(Commanding 34th Division, 1915-16)

[*To face p.* 54.

A PORTION OF THE LINE 55

Wez Macquart, a little further along, was in the Boche lines. A railway line ran from Armentieres through our lines into the Boche lines, and there were numerous roads which crossed No-Man's-Land. A considerable number of farmhouses were scattered along the roads in our area, which were utilised either for the gunners' accommodation or as observation posts, and those further back as Infantry billets for Battalions in support. Deep trenches were impossible, water being so near the surface, and the trenches were therefore breastworks similar to those we found in the area we previously held. There were four or five communication trenches leading up from our reserve line to the support of the front trenches.

CHAPTER VIII

CAMOUFLAGE MADE A FINE ART

THE Brigade soon settled into the regular trench routine. It was a comparatively quiet part of the line, though there were two salients on our side upon which the Boche frequently directed a very destructive fire, and always on these occasions caused us a certain amount of casualties. One of these points was in the right half of our sector and the other in our left. Owing to the wet, repairs were difficult. They could usually be only carried out at night, and the work was frequently again destroyed the next day. The garrisons of these points had a most unpleasant time of it, and it became necessary to relieve them more frequently than those of the remainder of our line who had comparative ease so far as the enemy fire was concerned. There were at that time no light trolley lines in use, and the carrying up of the R.E. materials from the reserve to the front trenches was a very arduous business. There was also an apparent shortage of materials, and it became difficult to obtain more than a small proportion of the stuff asked for. Major-General Ingouville-Williams and his senior general staff officer, Lieutenant-Colonel Mangles, inspected the trenches frequently. They were both well acquainted with this area, as General Williams' former Brigade had previously held this same bit of the line, and Lieutenant-Colonel Mangles had been his Brigade Major. Though matters had much improved as regards the supply of artillery ammunition there was still at this time need for economy in expenditure, so that the straffing of the

Boche was very limited compared to what became possible at a later date, and raids by our Infantry supported by Artillery were not organised as they were a few months later. We had some very inferior trench mortars of various types, and some few hand grenades, but rifle and machine gun fire was the main factor. Stokes mortars, and a liberal supply of hand and rifle grenades, and an unlimited quantity of shells for guns of all calibres came later on. After the Brigade had been in the line for some weeks it was relieved by the 103rd Brigade, and we went into billets at Erquinghem. Our losses had not been very serious, but still we had lost some valuable officers and men. Armentieres is, or was, a considerable town with wide streets of large residential houses as well as good shops, and at that time had suffered little from the enemy fire. The railway station was a wreck, and a certain number of houses had been destroyed, especially those on the outskirts of the town to the east, but the bulk of the place was intact. It was possible to buy almost anything in the town, and one or two restaurants did a good trade.

While we were in Divisional Reserve at Erquinghem, Colonel Elphinstone, Colonel Sillery, Major Soutry, and I occasionally lunched together in Armentieres, and the officers generally were glad to be able to get away sometimes for an hour or two from their Battalions. The meals supplied at the restaurant were surprisingly good and cheap. While the Division was holding this part of the line, nothing in the way of fighting on a large scale occurred. The Brigades took it in turns to hold the front line, and when not there remained in billets at Erquinghem, where musketry, bayonet exercise, and bomb-throwing were practised. The enemy did occasionally drop a few shells near the village, but it was generally with the intention of putting out of action a very heavy gun which was mounted on a railway truck and which every now and then stirred up the Boches in billets far in the rear of their lines. By the time the Boche began to fire the gun had moved away, so that it was never hit, but some of the houses in Erquinghem suffered. One of our Battalions when in support had a few men in a billet just outside Armentieres, and on one occasion when our anti-aircraft guns were shelling a Hun aeroplane, a shell case dropped through a roof of a house and fell on a man who was asleep in a room below and decapitated him. He was one of our first volunteers, a miner with five children, and it seemed hard that he should be knocked out in such an inglorious way; it might have occurred in London.

One minor incident of this time always sticks in my memory. I was walking along the front trench one day in order to watch the results of a small Artillery straf which we had arranged, and had taken up my position at a bit of the parapet, which was clear of lean-to's, when the enemy began a fusillade on that bit of our parapet with whizz-bangs which they kept up for a few minutes. These small shells travel fast, but do not penetrate a thick parapet. While I was sitting on the fire step waiting for the end of it, a shell struck the roof of a "lean-to" close by. I had previously seen an oldish man sitting in it smoking a clay pipe, gazing out evidently wrapped in thought, so I went over to see if he was all right. The shell had neatly removed with a great clatter and dust a number of sand-bags from the roof, leaving intact the corrugated iron sheeting which formed the ceiling about an inch over his head. The man was still sitting in the same attitude. I said I was glad to see that he was all right, and remarked that his roof had departed. "Ah weel, I hadn't obsarved it!" was all he said, which showed the depth of his reverie. Our Corps Commander was at this time Lieutenant-General Sir Charles Fergusson, who one day shortly after we arrived in the area called at the Brigade Headquarters while we were in the line, and it was arranged that on an

CAMOUFLAGE A FINE ART 59

early date he would inspect our trenches. It so happened that on the selected day the Boche was rather active, and the General was received with a certain amount of shell-fire. The Boche salute was again repeated upon his departure at the other end of the line, so that his visit was not entirely lacking in excitement. We were to again have the honour of serving under General Fergusson at a later date in one of the most successful operations in the course of the war, viz., at Arras, in April, 1917.

In order that the unit to which an officer or man belonged might be easily distinguishable some sort of badge on his khaki tunic was necessary. These marks were usually on the upper part of the sleeves or in the centre of the back below the collar.

After a conference of commanding officers on the subject when we were at Longbridge Deverill Camp, it was decided that our badge should consist of two diamond-shaped lozenges let into the tunic at the seams, joining the sleeve and the back. The 1st Battalion wore red diamonds, the 2nd yellow, the 3rd black, and the 4th blue. We found these badges answered the purpose admirably. There was also a Brigade badge, a thistle, painted on the transport wagons, with also a distinguishing St Andrew's Cross, painted in the colour of the Battalion to which the transport belonged, and each wagon was also adorned with the Divisional badge, which, in our case, was a black and white check pattern about a foot square. As each Division, Brigade, and Battalion in France had its distinctive badge, there was great diversity of colour and design. One soon got to know the badges of the Divisions round about. Every credit is due to the transport, as though by day they were camped some miles behind the lines, it was by no means a soft job, as every night they had to bring the rations and R.E. material up from the dumps in rear to the forward dumps close to the reserve line. This entailed the transport leaving their camp early in the afternoon, and they seldom returned to camp much before midnight. The weather was in winter bitterly cold or wet, and it frequently happened that the enemy opened fire on the wagons as they reached the forward dumps. The Boche knew our arrangements as regards such matters as well as we knew his, and both sides announced the fact occasionally. On the whole a transport man's existence was only just less unpleasant than that of his pals in the trenches.

One of the principal results of the cold and wet in the trenches was the disease known as trench feet. To guard against it the most stringent orders were issued by General Headquarters. Each man was held responsible, and was liable to heavy punishment in case of any infraction of the rules laid down to guard against the disease. Each man had to change his socks daily, and rub his feet well with whale oil. Company and Platoon Commanders were charged with the duty of assuring that the orders on the subject were strictly carried out. After a short time a case of trench feet became a rarity, and the admissions to hospital, at one time high, throughout the army, became almost negligible as regards trench feet.

The observation posts both of the gunners and of the Infantry were most mysterious spots; generally a house was selected as close to the front lines as possible, and to all appearances was nothing more than the usual ruin. No one was ever seen to approach it, and even from an aeroplane there was nothing to show that it was occupied. The doorways gaped open, and the windows were innocent of window frames; the roof had many gaps, and the outer walls were often more hole than wall. It would seem to the passer-by that there was nothing whatever to distinguish it from any other shattered house, but he would be wrong. There was a good deal of difference. Perhaps a tunnel ran underground for some distance with an entrance to the

CAMOUFLAGE A FINE ART

house cellar, a ladder fixed to the only corner of the ground floor room which was not seen from outside, might run up to a small wooden platform constructed on the rafters right under the tiled roof, sufficiently large for a man to sit on, and a little table just big enough to spread out a map on with a telephone adjacent. The man would be supplied with a telescope, and unseen would note through a space between the tiles all sorts of little things going on in the enemy's lines which would not otherwise have been observed, such as the flash showing the position of enemy guns, dust showing the movement of troops or transport on roads in rear, smoke coming from an apparently unoccupied ruin, unusual activity of any kind in the enemy's lines, and many such details. With the " squared " map in front of him he could, without loss of time, telephone the exact spot at which perhaps a body of troops was seen on the move to the Artillery who could, without seeing their target but using the map, open fire with often extremely unpleasant results to the unsuspecting Boches.

As time went on camouflage of observation posts became a fine art. A tree trunk about thirty feet high, the top and upper branches of which had been blown away by a shell, was found to be very suitable for this purpose. The most exact model of it with its jagged crown and small branches could be made in the camouflage workshop away back, and one night the real tree would be very carefully cut down and hidden in a ditch and the hollow metal painted model put up in its place. The next morning no change at all could be seen. These dummies were so well done that it was quite impossible at even a few yards' distance to distinguish the real from the copy. A small hole covered with camouflage bark admitted the observer, who, by climbing a ladder inside, obtained through a carefully concealed natural-looking crack in the rugged bark of the trunk, an excellent view over the enemy's lines at comparatively close range. There was such a tree put up in our lines about January, 1917, near Chappelle d'Armentieres which defied detection. It was one of a row of big trees growing along a ditch about four hundred yards from the front trench, and proved of great value to the local Intelligence Officers. These officers' duties comprised the daily collection and transmission to higher authority of all information collected in their area in the twenty-four hours. In a Brigade there was an officer usually selected from one of the Battalions and attached to the Brigade Staff who performed this duty. The staff of a Brigade was about this time also increased by the addition of officers attached, who acted as understudies of the Brigade Major and of the Staff Captain. They also at first came from the establishment of one of the Battalions, but later on were generally taken from some other Brigade in the same Division. This arrangement was excellent from a staff point of view, as should anything happen to one of the staff his place could be filled temporarily at any rate, by his more or less trained understudy. The Battalion Commanders were, however, not so well pleased, as they usually lost the services of some of their best officers, and as a large number of officers were always absent from a Battalion attending courses in signalling, bombing, trench mortars, and numerous other subjects, the Battalions were much under officered, and platoons were often commanded by N.C.O.'s. It was, of course, recognised that this condition was quite unavoidable, but a certain amount of good-natured grumbling on the part of C.O.'s was not unexpected, and the Tyneside Scots were much like other units in this respect.

CHAPTER IX

THE TRENCH "GARRISONS"

THE great Intelligence Department at General Headquarters was not, of course, dependent on the efforts of the front line Intelligence Officers for their information, which was supplied by our aeroplanes and agents living in the enemy's lines and cities on their lines of communication. Useful information was also obtained from prisoners captured in raids. Sometimes it was known that a change of troops holding the enemy's trenches had been made in a certain area, but the exact Divisions or Brigades comprising the new troops in the line were doubtful. In this case a raid would be organised with the primary object of obtaining this information either by the capture of prisoners or by cutting off the shoulder badges of Boches who had been killed in the raid. The Tyneside Scots in the winter of 1916-17 carried out many raids, but at the time I am now referring to, viz., the early spring of 1916, comparatively little was attempted in that line. The main feature of life in the trenches at Armentieres in the winter was the rain and the mud. The officers and men had a most disgusting time of it. It was one perpetual battle with slime. I found it hard work even to get round the trenches in the morning when the portions of the route which had pulverised in the night had been as a rule at least partly repaired; even then one got wet to the skin and caked with mud from head to foot. On one's return to Brigade Headquarters it was possible at any rate to get a bath and a change of kit, but the conditions under which the officers and men lived in the trenches was a thousand times worse.

They lived for five days and nights at a time, an existence only suited to the fauna of some cold mud world. It would have been an impossible existence had it not been for the close vicinity of the Boche, whose presence gave that touch of interest to life which made it just bearable. The Boche, of course, did his best to make things as uncomfortable as possible, and one of his little tricks was to dam up a certain stream which ran across No-Man's-Land from his line to ours, and suddenly release the water, which promptly flooded parts of our trenches and undermined our parapet. Pumps were always going, but they had but little effect. The land is so flat that the water would not run away; it meant merely pumping from one shell-hole into another. We were in a worse position than the enemy as his trenches being on a slope drained down to ours, and we were practically on a swamp and unable to get rid of the water. The snipers had perhaps a better time than the rest of the men; their duty was to lie hidden in a camouflaged loophole running through the parapet like a small tunnel, or on a roof, or up a tree, and watch for any Boche who incautiously showed himself, and bowl him over. Some of our men became very expert at this work. I remember on one occasion I came to a bay in the trench in which was a sniper's loophole, and found the four or five men, the occupants of the bay, doubled up with laughter on the fire step. It appeared that during the previous night our Artillery had knocked down a bit of the Boche front breast-work, leaving a gap of several yards. At daylight our snipers were keeping a cat-like watch on this point when they suddenly saw to their surprise a tall Boche walk slowly across the gap carrying a heavy plank on his head; he was closely followed by a much shorter Boche. They both evidently were quite unaware that they were exposing themselves, and stood still to talk in the middle of the

THE TRENCH "GARRISONS"　65

gap. One of our snipers thereupon drew a bead on the tall man, the range was only about two hundred yards, and fired. The tall Boche threw up his hands and fell down, the plank dropping on the head of the small man, knocking him down; the little man, thinking himself the victim of clumsiness on the part of his companion, got up, and rubbing his head stood still in the gap cursing and gesticulating at his recumbent friend. Then he suddenly bent forward, looked at him, seemed to grasp what had happened, gave a yell and bolted out of sight. The men in our bay had enjoyed the whole performance through crevices left in the top sand-bags, and said with tears in their eyes that it was as good as a pantomime. I asked the sniper why he had not polished off the little Boche too, and he said apologetically that he had tried to get a bead on him but had shaken so much with laughter that he could not manage it. The repairs of the Boche trench were subsequently postponed till dark and no further chances were given at that gap.

While the Boche was apparently plentifully supplied with gas, we were fortunate to escape it, though a certain number of gas shells were occasionally fired into our lines. Every man and officer was, of course, supplied with a gas mask, the pattern of which was later much improved, and gas mask drill was thoroughly practised by all ranks. Six seconds was, so far as I recollect, the time laid down for the adjustment of a gas mask. One always carried one, and if the wind was blowing from the enemy's lines towards ours, the mask was carried in such a way as to be very readily adjusted. At various points throughout each area signboards were put up, usually close to a sentry post, which showed whether the gas alert was on or not. If it were "on" it was imperative that every officer and man in that area wore his mask at the "ready." When the warning "Gas alert" was given, it remained in force until orders to the contrary were received from the Division, which

E

certainly occasionally led to the alert being kept up in the teeth of a gale blowing from us to the Boches, but was on the whole a safe arrangement.

The inhabitants of the trenches were by no means confined to humans. There were, in fact, three garrisons—the men, the rats, and the lice, and the two latter could by no means be overlooked though everything possible was done to discourage them. The legions of rats lived well and joyously. Not only were there innumerable fragments of honest meals to be easily found by the fattest and laziest, but other and more succulent fare was always available in No-Man's-Land and in the trenches, but slightly below the surface. The result was that the rat residents had the time of their lives, and thrived and multiplied to an unbelievable degree. At night in the trenches rats in some areas abounded to such an extent that they got under one's feet and were frequently trodden upon, and even by day they ran about as if the place belonged to them. They did much damage to boots, clothes, and equipment while the lawful owner slept in them. In one case an officer on awakening found that every one of the bone buttons on his clothes had been chawed off by rats while he rested for a few hours in the night. Many rats were killed, but still they increased, and I should imagine that the peasant farmers of the land in which the old lines of trenches were situated will have to take very thorough and drastic measures to deal with the plague or the damage to crops will be enormous. It was practically impossible to deal with the lice; the trenches themselves were full of them. Every man on coming out of the line was, however, marched to the baths especially erected in each area, where he was adequately treated and was given a complete clean outfit of clothing, so that while he was out of the line he was clean and free from vermin. His old clothing was cleaned and disinfected, and re-issued in due course to other bathers.

Night in the trenches was the time when the bulk

THE TRENCH "GARRISONS" 67

of the repairs to the trenches and dugouts was attended to, when the digging of new trenches was done, when the rations and R.E. materials were carried up, when patrols were sent out, and when raids took place. It was much more lively in the trenches by night than by day. Anything might happen, and in order to prevent anything in the way of a surprise by the enemy light was thrown on to No-Man's-Land by the use of a kind of Roman candle, numbers of which were fired at intervals at various spots along the front trench. These things were fired up in the air from a hand pistol, and were known as Very lights. Both sides used them. They went up, perhaps, a hundred yards and burnt a clear white light which lasted about a minute, and clearly showed up No-Man's-Land for a distance of a couple of hundred yards. The Boches used a prodigious number of these, at least three to every one of ours, and he also indulged in an occasional extra powerful light which, with a parachute fixed to it, brilliantly illuminated No-Man's-Land for several minutes as it slowly floated away. When we raided the Boche trenches, which we did with great frequency at a later period, the occasion was always marked by a really fine prototechnic display in his lines, rockets of various colours soared upwards, huge quantities of Very lights went up, elaborate strings of green or other coloured lights floated about, and one would have supposed that a Boche benefit was going on, the whole accompanied by the crashing of our guns, and the rattle of rifles and machine guns, all of which suddenly turned a peaceful night into a thunderous pandemonium increased by the incessant flashes and reports of bursting shells. A fine sight indeed, and one to enjoy if one could forget the toll we must pay and the gaps in the roll call to follow.

There is a certain staid and senior officer, a survivor of the original Tyneside Scots, who has cause to remember Very lights, though I am afraid to the rest of us the incident referred to was a source of considerable mirth. It appeared that on retiring to his virtuous couch for an hour or two's well-earned rest one wet night in the front trench outside Armentieres, he placed his lighted candle on a shelf in his dugout, on which, forgotten by him, reposed a Very light, and he went to sleep. Reliable eye-witnesses relate that suddenly the dark night was turned into day by an immense volume of white light and smoke pouring from a dugout near-by, out of which was seen to emerge with the greatest velocity a burning human form who flashed past, and, to their amazement, plunged with a yell and a splash into the chill depths of an overflowing shell hole near-by. It was a startling incident even to people accustomed to nightmares in real life and many a strange spectacle, and at first it was taken for granted that the conflagration was due to some unusual machinations on the part of our neighbours living opposite. It appeared, however, upon investigation that upon this occasion the Boche had nothing to do with it. The candle when it had burnt down had quietly ignited its neighbour the Very light, and the latter had acted as might be expected with the most startling results to the sleeper who, waking up and finding himself apparently in Hades, had successfully effected his escape, fortunately but little the worse.

I think it was some time in April (I have no written notes, and a very defective memory) that the order came for the Division to move into a back area for a short rest to be followed by "training." As was usual we had no idea as to our destination nor was any information given us as to our subsequent employment. The Tyneside Scottish were to be relieved by an Australian Brigade who were going into the line for the first time, at any rate, in that area. The Brigadier came to see me, and I gave him all the information I could concerning the local conditions, and the next night the relief took place, and was carried out

THE TRENCH "GARRISONS"

without any sort of contretemps. There was no hitch at all, and at 9 p.m., so far as all four of our Battalions and three of the Australians were concerned, the usual telephone reports from each unit had been received, "Relief complete," but though all seemed to be correct I did not care to leave until we had duly received a message from the Australian unit which had not reported, and was one of the two detailed to take over the front line trenches. The message from this unit seemed to be unaccountably delayed and we wondered what had happened. The Australian Brigadier and his Brigade Major and Major Soutry and myself talked and waited until past ten, when I ventured to suggest that some inquiry should be made as to the cause of the delay. The Brigade Major was accordingly sent to the telephone office in the next building to make inquiries. A few minutes later he reappeared with the missing telephone report. He reported to his Brigadier that on entering the telephone office, which was now being worked by the Australian Brigade signallers, he saw the message lying on the table, picked it up and read it. He asked the operator why the —— this message had not been delivered, and the indignant reply was "Oh, I'm fed up with writing 'Relief complete.' I've sent on a heap of 'em all the same and thought you had enough!" One could not help smiling, but I gathered that the Brigadier would have something to say on the morrow.

CHAPTER X

THE TRENCH MORTAR BATTERIES

The Brigade had had quite enough of the trenches for a time, and we were all of us glad of a rest, so that the march to the back area was hailed with satisfaction by all ranks. Officers and men would once again be able to sleep under a roof if, as was usually the case, that meant only on straw in a barn, and the miseries of trench life would cease for a while. The contrast made the march seem a picnic, and though the weather was bad and the men were often drenched to the skin and suffered many minor discomforts, they were in the highest spirits and thoroughly enjoyed the change. The Battalions, headed by their pipes, swung along merrily through the tumble-down villages, some of which we had passed through on our way up to the line; the smoking field-kitchens following with the dinners cooking, and the transport bringing up the rear. The Brigade on the march occupied about three miles of road, and was usually scattered for the night among three or four adjacent villages, to join up the next day on the road under a carefully worked-out time-table. These " march tables " were sometimes quite complicated affairs, owing to certain roads being blocked for a time by troops marching across them, and, therefore, only available for a certain few hours. Many a time have I seen our Brigade Major wrinkling his brow in the efforts to fit in the moves of the units to suit the time requirements. At night the Brigade Headquarters was sometimes in a more or less commodious château, and at others in a ramshackle

A Village in France.

[To face p. 70.

TRENCH MORTAR BATTERIES

farmhouse. The Battalion Headquarters were usually in one of the latter, and the junior officers might get a bed in a house or a shake-down in a barn. The men's accommodation was almost invariably straw in a farm building. The dinners were as a rule eaten during the midday halt.

A village in this particular part of France appears to consist of an aggregation of small farmhouses occupied by families who own or till the fields round about. The farm buildings, each enclosing its central pit, adjoin each other and run along both sides of the road and so form a street of farms, generally a very unsavoury one to the olfactory organs. The houses are mostly built of wooden framework filled in with mud, and frequently in urgent need of repair. Sanitation appears to be looked upon as superfluous, and the conditions of life generally seemed to be much behind those of an English village. The cattle are stall fed; one seldom sees any grazing. In each village are one or more seedy-looking estaminets where the villagers obtain their beer and sit and chat, and there are usually one or two brick or stone rather showy-looking small villas built and occupied by the Mayor or Notary. On the outskirts of the village there is frequently a château, in generally a more or less dilapidated condition, surrounded by neglected grounds which is inhabited by an old family not infrequently of the same name as the village. An extremely dirty pond covered with green slime, and surrounded by rough grass full of empty tins and broken crockery, seemed to be the common adjunct of each village. One would gather that such a squalid life as the villagers seem to lead must be the result of extreme poverty, but on the contrary it is stated that the thrift of the peasantry is extraordinary, and that many a hoard of money is hidden in the mean-looking dwellings. If so, it seems to be thrift carried to excess. Of course, during the war no young men were to be seen in the villages; they were all serving in the army, so that the farm work was entirely carried on by women, boys, girls, and old men, who worked hard early and late, and with such success that the amount of land not under cultivation appeared to be very little.

The roads, usually good in France, had suffered much from the war, more especially those in this part of the country. The constant wear and tear of guns and heavy motor lorries had reduced many of them to little better than cart tracks pitted with holes a foot deep, full of mud and water in wet weather and dust in dry. The central portion of the main roads is, however, paved with stone, and remained in fairly good order; so long as a wagon remained on the *pavé* there was no trouble, but if, owing to careless driving or accident, a wheel left the *pavé* it often sank into the mud up to its axle, and the wagon had to be unloaded before it could proceed, perhaps causing serious delay and congestion of traffic in rear. At all cross roads military police were stationed to regulate the traffic. In some areas this duty was carried out admirably; in others the want of proper supervision of the road traffic was very noticeable. Repairs to roads were by no means neglected, large numbers of men being continually at work on them; it was largely due to the efforts of the labour Battalions that the roads survived. Everyone who has been in France will have been impressed with the immense amount of traffic which the roads had to sustain owing to the conditions of modern warfare, the huge size of the forces employed and to be maintained, and consequently the gigantic amount of supplies of all kinds requiring transport. The railways by themselves would have been quite inadequate to the needs of the army and civil population, and though special railway lines were built to ease the situation the railways alone would still have been quite insufficient had they not been supplemented by road vehicles on an enormous scale. The numbers of heavy motor lorries and buses employed must

TRENCH MORTAR BATTERIES 73

have run into scores of thousands. The buses were used to carry troops, and the lorries rations and ammunition. The remarkable verbs to "embus" and to "debus" had to be invented to meet the requirements of written or verbal orders for troops detailed to use buses, and presumably will survive for use in future campaigns.

The swift transfer of considerable bodies of troops from one part of the battle front to another by motor transport was one of the special features of this campaign.

Our march occupied eight days, and we were very pleased to find that the country round about the villages in which our Battalions were to be billeted was very different from the uninteresting, low-lying flats which we had left. Here we found undulating country prettily wooded, and a better class of farm. The cottages had a much more civilised appearance with small, well-kept gardens gay with spring flowers. The Brigade Headquarters was established in a very comfortably furnished house, with an office in an adjacent building. A small stream ran along the opposite side of the road fringed with willow trees just breaking out into spring green. The weather became bright and warm, and life took on a very different aspect. The various Battalions were also comfortably housed. Sillery's Headquarters were about two miles away, at Recques, in a charming old house, a sort of farm château with an old world garden and park. The men were billeted in barns on the property and in the village close by. Elphinstone, with the 3rd Battalion, was in a rather large farmhouse at Nortleulinghen, Dunbar-Stuart and the 2nd Battalion in the village of Nordasques, and Lyle with the 4th Battalion at Bayenghem.

After a rest of a day or two training began, and the clothing and equipment was thoroughly overhauled and deficiencies were rapidly made good. Each unit constructed extempore rifle ranges in disused quarries or other suitable spots for musketry practice, and classes for bomb-throwing, bayonet fighting, signalling, machine gunnery, trench mortars, etc., were soon in full swing. Officers and men smartened themselves up, the transport wagons were repainted (most of them required it badly), and the appearance generally of the Brigade underwent a remarkable change. In a very few days signs of trench life had gone, weary looks had disappeared, and the Brigade was as smart and gay as ever. The Divisional Headquarters were at Tilques, and General Williams often paid us visits of inspection, and he often said how pleased he was with the Brigade and how glad he was to have them in his Division, and that he recognised the thoroughly soldierly spirit animating all ranks. As we had received drafts from our home depot our ranks were again up to establishment. All were Tyneside Scots, and every officer and man of the 4,000 in the Brigade had one solid and fixed idea in common, and that was that the Tyneside Scottish Brigade was of all Brigades the best and finest. This clan feeling, or esprit de corps, was a magnificent asset of incalculable value to a fighting force, and one to be encouraged in every possible way. All was well with the Brigade, and we did our best to get to the top notch of preparation in the time at our disposal for the tussle with the Boches, which we vaguely knew could not be far off. We were really preparing for the great struggle which was to come in July, and which was to be known in history as the Battle of the Somme.

Major Soutry—or while he was away on short leave, his understudy, Major Mackintosh—and I spent much of our time riding round and watching the training in progress. I personally always look back upon this period in the back area as a sort of "time" oasis full of pleasant memories of friends one was alas! destined so soon to lose. It was the lull before the storm. After perhaps a fortnight of company and Battalion training,

TRENCH MORTAR BATTERIES 75

Divisional and Brigade exercises commenced, and consisted mainly of the practice of the "attack" on an imaginary enemy's position. A suitable piece of country for the practice was selected by the Divisional Commander. The Brigade happened to be a good many miles from the place of assembly, so that on these occasions a very early start was necessary, and by the time the Brigade had got back again to their billets some Battalions had covered over twenty miles of road and across rough ploughed land, a good test of their marching powers. It was about the end of April when the Division was ordered to move up into the area behind Albert. We were to proceed by rail, and soon found ourselves in the neighbourhood of Amiens, and marched from that point eastwards. The temporary destination of Brigade Headquarters was Franvillers, and the Brigade was billeted in that and neighbouring villages about seven miles south-west of Albert. The country round here is undulating and highly cultivated; numerous small villages are scattered about at short distances apart, so that there was no lack of billets for officers and men. The Brigade Headquarters was lucky in finding comfortable quarters in a small furnished house in the main street, and we were in a few hours in telephone communication with the Division and the various units of the Brigade.

Our Brigade signalling section, under Lieutenant Dowse, was always uncommonly smart about this. Wherever we went they lost no time in getting telephone temporary lines laid, though I gathered that it was not always easy to persuade the O.C. Divisional Signalling Company to part with the necessary material. Dowse, however, was a most ingenious and quick-witted young officer, never at a loss on difficult occasions, and he was lucky to have to deal with exceptionally efficient Battalion signalling officers who were more than ready to do their share: the results were excellent. It was most satisfactory to know that our signalling arrangements were in such thoroughly capable hands, and that should, from shelling or other causes, an interruption occur, one might safely count on the necessary repairs to the wires being carried out in record time. In the back area such interruptions were occasional, and were the result of ordinary accidents to the temporary lines which were often festooned along the tops of hedges and carried on rough poles or on trees across roads, but in the trench area the wires were perpetually in need of repair, as, though they were usually laid along one side of the communication trenches and so were protected to some extent, they suffered much from shell-fire, and were often broken by carrying parties struggling up the trenches in the dark. After a time the numbers of wires, old and new, to be seen in the trenches to the layman in electrical matters seemed remarkable, as in addition to the Infantry wires there were wires in use for the Artillery, and also a number of lengths of wire that were out of date and useless. I must admit it was always somewhat of a mystery to me that the signallers could ever find the particular wire out of the maze that they wanted, but they certainly did manage to do so most satisfactorily. From time to time old wires were collected in parts of the line, and labels with mystic symbols were affixed at intervals to the lines in use showing to the initiated the particular branch to which it belonged, and various other bits of information. Heavy shelling would, however, sadly interfere with all these excellent arrangements, so that the repair work of the signalling section never ceased.

While our headquarters were at Polincove in the back area I took the opportunity of motoring over one day to Estaples to have a look at the reinforcements collected there for the Brigade, and found a very useful lot. They had since then joined us. The 3rd Battalion had been for some

TRENCH MORTAR BATTERIES

time short of a second-in-command, and the vacancy was now filled up by the appointment of Major S. Acklom, a regular officer, but who had been serving during the war with the Glasgow Highlanders. He soon proved himself to be a valuable acquisition to his Battalion and to the Brigade, and greatly distinguished himself later on. In addition to the four Infantry Battalions we had a trench mortar Battery manned by officers and men from units in the Brigade, and commanded by Lieutenant E. F. Bowkett. This Battery was armed with, I think it was four Stokes mortars, an extremely simple form of mortar. It consisted of a cylinder about three feet long, and when in action was fixed to an iron stand plate and elevated to an angle of about forty-five degrees. At the bottom of the cylinder is a pin, the shell is dropped in by hand, and a cap in its base striking upon the pin, ignites the propelling charge which is contained in the base of the shell itself. The action of loading being so simple, shells can be fired practically as fast as they can be dropped into the muzzle, and though the shells are small and the range not great, a tremendous amount of damage can be done in a very short time to the enemy's trenches and their inhabitants. These early pattern Stokes guns were of small calibre, but at a later date larger ones were made. The Infantry, however, did not have to deal with the large Stokes which were apportioned to the Artillery.

On the march the Stokes guns were trundled along on hand carts, rope-pulled by their teams, and as they were necessarily loaded up with the teams' packs, etc., the general effect was anything but smart, rather reminding one in fact of broken-down coster barrows. However, there was no help for it, and whatever was deficient in the appearance of the Battery on the move was amply made up by their fighting value in the trenches and the gallantry displayed by the teams. The trench mortar Battery was in trench warfare no doubt easily the most unpopular of all branches with both friend and foe. Its friends had no desire whatever to retain its company, as immediately a mortar opened fire that part of the trench at once became the target of the enemy's most pronounced retaliation of which the Infantry in the vicinity got the unwelcome benefit. The mortar teams stuck to their work under a hail of fire of all kinds of projectiles in a way which never failed to extort the unbounded, if disguised, admiration of their Infantry comrades who, however, could well have dispensed with their proximity. I think of all the jobs in the trenches which demanded pluck, determination, and staying power of the highest order, there were none to surpass the trench mortar Battery work. It was not surprising that the casualties in the Battery were very high. I always had the very highest admiration for the little group of officers and men who formed our Brigade Trench Mortar Battery, and did such magnificent work. Lieutenant Bowkett belonged to the 2nd Battalion, and was especially selected for the appointment. He had, while we were previously in the trenches outside Armentieres, distinguished himself on several occasions by his daring patrol work, which had been of great value in connection with various small raids which we had carried out, and at a later date was again to distinguish himself on the Somme.

Up till now there had been a certain number of "Lewis" machine guns in possession of each Battalion, and this number had been gradually increased until it eventually amounted to one gun to each platoon, viz., sixteen to each Battalion. At the same time a new unit had been added to each Infantry Brigade, the Machine Gun Company. It was armed with sixteen "Vickers" machine guns, and was fully equipped with horsed limbers, and able to move at a good pace. Our Machine Gun Company was commanded by Captain N. C. Ingpen, and consisted of roughly a dozen officers and something under two hundred men. The

TRENCH MORTAR BATTERIES

Vickers gun is somewhat heavier than the Lewis gun, and is very suitable for firing from fixed positions in rear over the heads of the Infantry, stationary or advancing, whereas the Lewis is very portable and can be easily carried forward by Infantry advancing and used with effect in the front line in an attack. They can both fire at the rate of anything up to four hundred rounds a minute. Our " Lewis " guns were usually distributed along the front trench and fired over the top of the parapet. The " Vickers " were usually divided, half in the front trenches and half in the reserve line, and were posted in carefully concealed " Battle stations " which were concreted gun positions at important points, either, if in the front trenches, to bring a cross fire to bear in front of a salient jutting out from our line, or if in the rear, to command certain of our communication trenches which the enemy would probably use in his advance should he succeed in breaking through our front line; or to sweep open spaces over which the Boches would have to move in the same contingency. The Vickers guns were never allowed to fire from their Battle positions so as not to disclose their positions to the Boche, but were daily and nightly fired from other points sometimes in conjunction with a raid or an Artillery straf, or in the common everyday work of harassing the enemy, particularly his communication trenches.

It soon became known that we, as we expected, were to take part in a big simultaneous attack on several miles of the enemy's trenches, and that our particular job would be to assault that part of the enemy's line running from a point about eight hundred yards north to five hundred yards south of the village of La Boisselle, which was situated just inside his line and lay across the main road leading from Albert to Bapaume. The 101st Brigade were to attack on our right, and the 103rd Tyneside Irish Brigade was to form reserves to both the leading Brigades. On the left of our

Brigade another Division, the 8th, was to attack. In order that everyone concerned should understand as exactly as possible what had to be done, frequent practice attacks were organised by each of the Divisions concerned under the personal supervision of General Sir H. Rawlinson, commanding the 4th Army, and of our Corps Commander, Lieutenant-General Sir W. Pulteney. For our Division a piece of country in the neighbourhood of Franvillers was marked out with lines of different coloured flags to represent No-Man's-Land and the successive lines of enemy's trenches, and also his communication trenches. The village of Heilly was supposed to represent La Boisselle. There was a main road through it which corresponded roughly with the Albert-Bapaume road. Though there was really very little resemblance between the formation of the practice ground and that of the actual ground to be passed over in the real attack, still great benefit was gained by these rehearsals in many ways; the distances between the various objectives were correctly shown, the officers and men could form a good idea of the general requirements, and the numerous minor points which from time to time were found to require attention could be legislated for.

It was laid down that while our Brigade should attack both to the north and to the south of La Boisselle, the village itself should not be attacked frontally. It was a particularly strong point, and it was therefore considered that a direct assault would be very costly, and it was intended that our troops should, after passing the village on each side, close in and attack it from all sides at once. It followed that between the two Battalions of the Tyneside Scottish which were to attack to the north of La Boisselle and the two which were to attack to the south of it there was a gap of several hundred yards. Albert at this time was very largely already ruined by the enemy fire, the cathedral was a mere shell, and comparatively few

THE CATHEDRAL, ALBERT, 1916. [*To face p.* 80.

TRENCH MORTAR BATTERIES

houses remained quite intact, but a considerable number of troops were billeted fairly comfortably in the town, and one café, at least, was open where a meal could be obtained. The town lies in a hollow, and on the east was hidden from the direct observation of the Boches by a considerable ridge running in a north and south direction, the top of which was about two miles from the town. This ridge was occupied by the British, whose front trenches were at the foot of the further or eastward (the steeper) slope of the ridge, and faced the Boche front trench at a distance varying from fifty yards to eight hundred yards. The road from Albert to Bapaume ran from the town straight up over the top of the ridge down the eastern slope, across No-Man's-Land, and then up through the village of La Boisselle. The distance from the top of our ridge to our front trench at the bottom of the slope was about a thousand yards, and the intervening ground was cut up into a complicated mass of reserve, supports and communication trenches, some new, some old. The whole surface was a mass of shell-holes of various sizes, and the numbers of holes increased daily.

CHAPTER XI

THE BRIGADE HEADQUARTERS AT THE VILLA ROCHERS

In this part of the country the subsoil is chalk, so that the trenches and excavations of all kinds were clearly marked out in white, and any new trench was very noticeable. The Boche had, of course, accurate plans of our trenches, as we indeed had of his, both supplied by aerial photographs. These plans of the enemy's trenches were carefully kept up to date by the Intelligence Department, who supplied new ones to the troops from time to time. The French Army had at an earlier period of the war held this line, and had constructed a number of very deep dugouts in the trenches, some of which went down to a depth of thirty feet, and a few of them were large enough to hold fifty men. The majority were much smaller, but they were all of considerable depth, a great contrast to the inadequate shelters available in the Armentieres section of the line. There were numerous deep dugouts in our front trench, but it would have been impossible for the men to get out of them in time to repel a surprise raid; in fact, these dugouts would have proved mere traps, so their use was prohibited, and the entrances were closed up by a network of barbed wire. The deep dugouts in the supports and reserve trenches were, however, found most useful not only for the shelter of the garrisons of the trenches, but for use as advanced dressing stations, company and Battalion Headquarters, and signallers' dugouts, and for R.E. and ammunition dumps.

The narrowest bit of No-Man's-Land was that

THE VILLA ROCHERS

dividing our front trench from the Boche trench in front of the village of La Boisselle. Here it was barely fifty yards across, and the whole surface of the ground was a broken and confused jumble of mine craters. Both sides took advantage of the nature of the soil to sink shafts and throw out mining galleries, and explode mines under the trenches opposite. On our side there was no attempt to maintain anything approaching a regularly defined front trench immediately opposite the village; small detached posts at intervals of fifty yards or so had to suffice. The rest of the line was held in the usual way, with listening posts thrown out a short distance in front. The mining company of the R.E., who were working in our section of the line, did marvels, and completely outwitted the Boche. Prior to the 1st of July they had managed to complete two galleries right across No-Man's-Land, which were utilised on that date with startling results to the Hun, who, in spite of all his countermining efforts, was quite unaware of what was in progress. These tunnels were each about two hundred and fifty yards long and ended under the enemy's front trench, where two very strongly fortified and heavily garrisoned posts, one on each flank of the village of La Boisselle had been constructed. While No-Man's-Land between us and the village of La Boisselle was very narrow, its width increased rapidly to the north and south of the village. To the north it developed to a width of eight hundred yards, and to the south to two hundred and fifty, this being principally due to the fact that La Boisselle was built on a small spur forming a salient jutting out towards us with a valley on each side of it.

The valleys were named on our trench maps "Sausage" and "Mash" respectively. Of course, the village had really long since quite disappeared, and nothing but untidy heaps of rubble remained to mark the site, as was invariably the case with all villages and hamlets so unfortunate as to form part of the advanced battle area in trench warfare times. From our ridge we could get quite a good view into the ruins of the village, lying as it did much lower on the opposite side of the valley, along the bottom of which No-Man's-Land wound like a river; but the Boche was so well dug in that signs of life were very seldom visible, though we knew the place was crammed with troops. Our Artillery and machine guns often played on the ruins, and from time to time a concentrated Artillery straf of the village took place, but it is doubtful if many casualties even then resulted owing to the depths of the dugouts. The ground behind the enemy's front trench sloped upwards towards the plateau in the rear, on which nine miles away was the town of Bapaume. About a thousand yards to the north of La Boisselle was the village of Ovillers, which was just inside the Boche front trench. It was by now also a mere rubbish heap, but was very heavily fortified.

The left of our attack was to be delivered upon a point a little to the south of this village; our right, that is where we joined the 101st Brigade, was to be directed upon a point several hundred yards south of the southern end of La Boisselle. As the enemy had for many months past been busily engaged on the work of strengthening their defences along No-Man's-Land and in rear by every possible means in their power their trenches by this time had become almost of the nature of permanent fortifications. Strong barbed wire entanglements several yards wide formed a formidable barrier in front of the trenches, and other obstacles were plentiful, such as knife rests and ditches planted with sharp spikes. The parapets of the trenches gave a splendid field of Infantry fire, the trenches bristled with hundreds of machine guns cunningly hidden from view, even from the air, underground passages allowed of the unobserved passage of troops from one point to another, and batteries of guns of all calibres were so posted as

LA BOISSELLE FROM

THE VILLA ROCHERS

to do the utmost execution in case of an attack on our part. A projected advance by the British was no secret to the enemy, who were fully aware of our intentions. The concentration of vast numbers of troops in any given area takes time and cannot nowadays be entirely hidden from the enemy, owing to the facilities of observation by aeroplanes whose observers cannot fail to note the signs of preparations, such as the movements of troops and stores by rail and road, the formation of the main dumps, the laying down of light rails, the massing of guns, and the digging of trenches for reserve troops. Apart from the use of aeroplanes, spies also are always at work, and manage to keep the enemy well supplied with news of events which necessarily cannot be kept hidden from the knowledge of the inhabitants of the countryside, and are so far public property. Therefore it was not surprising that the Boche would know a great deal of what was going on in our lines, and would be prepared accordingly to give us a very warm reception.

Prisoners captured on the 1st of July stated that the troops had been warned of the exact date and time of the attack, but in view of the fact that, owing to unforeseen circumstances, the C.-in-C. had found it necessary to suddenly postpone the attack for forty-eight hours, it seems doubtful if the news of this postponement could have reached the enemy in time, but in any case they were quite ready when the time came. One of the points of vital importance to commanders in the field is the early and regular transmission of news from the troops advancing, to the authorities in rear. Without such early information a commander cannot form an opinion as to how matters are going, and is very much in the dark as to the requirements of the situation. Telephone wires are usually not immediately available, and "runners" are liable to casualties and delay. Though observers in aeroplanes can follow the movements of troops to a certain extent and give useful information, it was evident that much more detailed and accurate reports would be forthcoming if communication between the advanced troops and the aeroplanes could be arranged. A simple means by which troops could communicate by signal with the aeroplanes detailed for the particular purpose was accordingly instituted. Our rehearsals of the attack were always attended by especially detailed aeroplanes flying overhead, who from time to time picked up by signal messages from Brigade or Battalion Headquarters taking part in the advance. To help acquaint the aeroplane quickly of the identity of the sender a Brigade Headquarters was indicated by a large white sheet spread on the ground, and a Battalion Headquarters by a sheet of a different shape. The messages were signalled from the ground in code by means of a sort of venetian blind shutter which was laid flat on the ground, and was worked by a string; when the slats were closed they showed white and when open, black: a simple arrangement which was found to answer the purpose.

In order to allow the aeroplane to see for itself the exact positions reached by the leading line of Infantry, the latter was liberally provided with red flares which when lighted clearly indicated the extent of our advance to the aeroplane above. This information was particularly necessary to the Artillery in the rear, whose fire could then be accurately ranged with confidence that they were not shooting into our troops. Among the numerous and varied preparatory details, to which much time and attention had to be given prior to an advance in trench warfare, was the formation of numbers of ration, ammunition, and R.E. material dumps in the trenches from which the attack was to be made. These dumps contained all the more immediate requirements of the attacking force. Vast quantities of stores had to be conveyed from the Divisional dumps up the communication trenches, generally at night, to the advanced

THE VILLA ROCHERS

dumps by carrying parties of Infantry told off for this purpose. The work was heavy, and officers and men would have much preferred to spend their time in the front trenches, however unpleasant the Boche might make it. The various stores were deposited in the trenches in dugouts selected for the purpose. One of the most disliked duties was the carrying up of gas cylinders for installation in our front trench, where, from time to time, hundreds were planted under the parapet ready for use as soon as the wind should be favourable. Accidents from gas occasionally occurred to carrying parties, and enemy shells sometimes exploded the cylinders with fatal results to men in the vicinity.

On one occasion we lost seventeen men in our front trench owing to a shell having struck the parapet a short distance away, and though it did not hit the cylinder itself, the latter was bulged sufficiently to allow the gas to escape. The R.E. gas specialists spent days at a time at our Brigade Headquarters waiting for a suitable wind to allow of the gas being released. There was a general sigh of relief when we had got rid of the stuff. At a later date mortars were used which threw large cylinders of gas into the Boche lines. The base of these mortars were buried a short distance in the earth, and they were fired simultaneously, perhaps a hundred or more at a time, by electricity. We had a line of about four hundred of these mortars in our trenches at Arras, in 1917, and they were used to deluge with gas a particular spot in the Boche defences which required special attention. After the mortars had been fired there was no sign of them in view, the recoil having driven them out of sight into the soft ground. The range of these mortars was about one thousand yards. At Albert, in 1916, however, this form of retaliation on the Hun had not materialised, and we had to content ourselves with the release of gas which the wind blew from our trenches to theirs. The gas, being heavier than the air, having rolled across

No-Man's-Land and beyond, found its way into the enemy's trenches and dugouts, and any Hun caught before he could adjust his gas mask would not worry us any more. As a precaution against gas in our trenches numerous rough gongs made of a bit of railway iron (and at a later date sirens worked by compressed air) were installed each under a sentry whose duty it was to sound the gas alarm at the first sign of an enemy gas attack.

During the time that I served with the Brigade I cannot recollect any attempt at a serious gas attack on us, but we occasionally got whiffs which drifted to us from some more or less distant unit which was suffering from gas, and, of course, we did not escape the ordinary gas shells which the enemy favoured us with at intervals. After we had been at Franvillers for about a fortnight, we moved up to Albert, and relieved another Brigade in the trenches. Our front was on the left in touch with the 8th Division, and the 101st Brigade joined us on our right. The Albert-Bapaume Road ran through the centre of our Brigade lines. Our lines included Becourt Wood on our right, and extended northward for about one and a quarter miles, our left being opposite a point roughly halfway between La Boisselle and Ovillers. On the top of our ridge, which extended all along behind our trenches, two strongly organised little forts had been constructed, one between Becourt and the Bapaume road, and the other half a mile to the north of the road. These forts were known as the Usna, and Tara, redoubts, respectively, and were garrisoned by portions of Battalions in reserve. The château of Becourt was almost hidden in the wood, and had been a fine old country-house; it was now, however, much knocked about, and its private chapel was a ruin, but it made a useful headquarters for our right Battalion in support. The headquarters of the other three Battalions were accommodated in dugouts in the trenches. We had an arrangement that the 1st and 4th Battalions

THE VILLA ROCHERS

should as far as possible work together, and the same held good for the 2nd and 3rd Battalions, so that while the 1st and 2nd would be holding the front trenches they would be supported and subsequently relieved, respectively, by the 4th and 3rd. It was part of the duties of the Battalions in support to supply large working parties in the trenches, by day or by night, and the knowledge that their work would be to their own ultimate benefit was a useful incentive.

As time went on the Artillery straffing on both sides gradually became more severe and the casualties mounted up. Our night patrols in No-Man's-Land frequently came into contact with Boche patrols, and several minor raids attempted by the enemy were beaten off. Captain G. Charlton, 3rd Battalion, greatly distinguished himself in one of these fights. On one occasion the Huns organised a night attack by two Battalions supported by an Artillery bombardment on our trenches on the right, just in front of Becourt, which were held by the 2nd Battalion, and succeeded in penetrating some distance into our lines, behind our support trench before he could be stopped; but he was successfully driven out again with considerable losses by the 2nd and 3rd Battalions. Our trenches were well constructed, and unless a shell dropped right into a trench little damage was done. Sometimes when going round the trenches one would find that the Boche for some unapparent reason was obstinately maintaining a heavy fire on some particular bit of the defences which one wished to visit, and in that case one waited until the bombardment stopped; or it might happen that the trench one was in, was suddenly shelled, in which case I used to sit on the bottom of the trench and chat to the men who happened to be there, and smoke till we could move on again. The medical arrangements were excellently organised, and immediate attention was insured to the wounded; stretcher-bearers were on duty at certain points in the trenches, whose job it was to move the wounded at once to the nearest dressing station, usually a dugout in one of the communication trenches slightly in rear of the support line, where the Battalion medical officer and his assistant had their surgery. Here first aid was given, and the men were then carried down a communication trench to some spot in the reserve line where they were placed in ambulances and whisked off to a field hospital; and a man often found himself in a hospital in England in almost no time.

Everything occurred so rapidly that once an officer or man was wounded he seemed to vanish into space, so far as his unit was concerned, and generally nothing whatever was heard of him until he might be eventually heard of as either in or having been discharged from, one of the hospitals at home. This did not apply to the very slightly wounded who, after a short stay in a local field hospital, generally returned to their units; all other cases were evacuated to England, and when this was the case, they were on recovery available for posting to any Battalion at home or abroad. From our point of view this was by no means a satisfactory arrangement; we should have liked to have had our own officers and men sent back to us, but the exigencies of the service did not apparently permit of this being done. We, unfortunately, lost the services of many a good soldier in this way. The Brigade Headquarters was now in a small two-roomed house which formed part of the premises of extensive farm buildings known as Belle Vue, about a mile in rear of Becourt Château, the extreme right of our line. The enemy every now and then dropped shells near our abode which exploded as a rule without doing any particular damage. Though the place was dirty and inconveniently small, the principal objection was the distance from the centre and left of the Brigade trenches. It was, however, a pleasant enough ride up nearly to the top of the ridge, near the entrance

THE VILLA ROCHERS

to one or other of the communication trenches, where one dismounted and sent the horses to the rendezvous for the return trip, but a good deal of time was wasted.

Colonel Rundle, who was at that time in command of the Artillery in the Brigade area, and I used to have daily conferences at my headquarters in connection with the planning of strafs on the Boche trenches, and on one occasion he had just started to return to his headquarters when I happened to recollect some point which we had overlooked and sent out to ask him to return for a minute, which he did. He then left, and as he came close to his own shanty he saw a shell hit it and blow it to atoms. The fragments of the body of his orderly officer, who was in the hut at the time, had to be collected from the branches of a neighbouring tree. As Colonel Rundle explained to me the next day had he not been accidently delayed he would certainly have just reached the hut in time to be blown up, so he had a fortunate escape. At the end of a spell of some weeks in the trenches the Brigade was relieved and went into billets in Albert. It then formed part of the reserve which was available for reinforcing the trench garrisons should that be necessary. I had on a previous occasion noticed that a certain very nice-looking house at the eastern end of the town, enclosed in a charming garden, was not apparently being made much use of. On inquiry it appeared that one or two stray officers seemed to have established themselves there temporarily from time to time, but it was evident to me that it would make a very suitable Brigade Headquarters for the Tyneside Scottish. It was centrally situated as regards our Battalions, and there was ample accommodation for the staff. The house was extremely comfortably furnished; an elderly woman caretaker was in charge, and one of the gardeners still looked after the garden which was shady and bright with flowers. The name of the place was the Villa

Rochers. The necessary permission having been obtained, this villa now became for a time our headquarters. The caretaker proved herself to be an excellent cook, and we slept in luxurious beds in rooms evidently furnished by Paris firms, and ate our meals in a delightful kind of winter garden or, if we preferred, in a well-furnished dining-room. It was amusing to see the surprised looks of most of our visitors who were evidently secretly eaten up with jealousy, while we pretended to be used only to Brigade Headquarters of this class, but matters became serious when various visiting potentates cast an obviously envious eye on our surroundings.

General Williams was himself installed with his headquarters' staff in a comfortable house two or three miles in rear, and horrified me by suggesting that the Château Rochers would make an excellent Divisional Headquarters. The idea, however, was, we were gratified to hear, vetoed by the Corps Commander on the grounds that the villa was in too advanced a position for the purpose. Just as we had begun to breathe afresh a series of officers of senior rank came to see the place, and asked a number of questions, and it was difficult to persuade some of them that the villa was really not what they required. The casual reference to the damage, some only imaginary, daily caused by shell fire often had a valuable effect. One day a Brigadier, sent as an emissary of the commander of the 5th Army (the reserve army), arrived, and I gathered that there was some idea of utilising the villa at some future time as an advanced battle position for the general staff of that army, and in that case preparations would be necessary which would entail our turning out. I never clearly quite understood the object of this visit, but whatever was the intention our visitor departed and we heard no more. The Corps Commander, however, caused us serious alarm as he seemed much taken with the house, perhaps as an advanced Battle

THE VILLA ROCHERS

station, and having inspected it pretty closely held a mysterious conversation with the staff officer who was with him. After a few days we found a party of sappers very busily engaged in digging a trench in the garden, and laying a cable which they stated was to be utilised by the Corps Commander! This certainly did look serious, but in the end we were left in peace until the Brigade moved once more into the trenches, and the Brigade Headquarters was installed in all the magnificence of a dugout. I shall always have pleasant recollections of the Villa Rochers. It was there that so many of our friends came to accept our very modest hospitality, and in too many cases, alas, for the last time. It is not difficult now to picture the frequent " pow-wows " held in the winter garden, General Williams sitting at the head of the large table with the Brigadiers, C.O.'s, and staff officers grouped round it.

These conferences dealt with the arrangements for the coming attack, and embraced a very large number of subjects, ranging from the details of the Artillery barrage down to the exact manner in which an Infantry man should carry a spade. No point was too small to be thrashed out, and the conferences usually beginning at 8 p.m. seldom closed before midnight, which, however, was not altogether a matter of congratulation to officers who had appointments at early dawn. The caretaker was a plucky old woman full of hatred and scorn of the Boche. The house and gardens had been hit by shells pretty often, and I asked what she did when the place was shelled, to which she replied, " If it's just the ordinary shelling, I take no notice, but if it's a bombardment I go *la bas*," pointing to the cellars, one of which she had fitted up very comfortably as a bedroom. Her husband, an old man, she had not seen or heard of since the outbreak of war, when unhappily he had been visiting relations at a village east of Bapaume. She had no idea of what his or their fate had been or whether he was alive or dead, and one could fully sympathise with her when she forcibly and fluently expressed her feelings towards *les salles Boches*. I forget exactly what she considered an adequate fate for the Kaiser, should he fall into our hands, but " boiling oil " would be comparatively mere child's play.

CHAPTER XII

THE ROAR OF A BOMBARDMENT

I THINK it was about the 7th June that we moved into the trenches again and took over the same section as before. The Brigade Headquarters, however, was to remain at the Château Rochers until the time should come when it could move into a dugout which the R.E. were constructing for our use in a new line of trench dug by the Infantry, joining up the two forts, Usna and Tara. It was intended that we should move into this the day previous to that on which the preliminary Artillery bombardment was to begin. Meanwhile, the work in the trenches was very much as before, but carrying parties were kept particularly busy day and night under the supervision of Captain Wallace Marrs, our Staff Captain, in stocking the various advanced dumps in our area. The amount of stores to be carried up was large. There were R.E. material, such as coils of barbed wire, iron stakes, mallets, sand-bags and entrenching tools, rations, water, hand grenades, and ammunition. The loads had each to be made up into suitable sizes and weights to be carried by one man. These stores were not for use in our present trenches, but were to be carried forward by hand immediately in the rear of the advancing Infantry by especially organised carrying parties, each of which consisted of thirty men under an officer. Each carrying party was to carry a proportion of each sort of store.

As soon as the leading lines of Infantry had reached their objectives in the attack they would at once set to work to " consolidate " their positions, utilising for this purpose the R.E. stores brought up to them by the carrying parties. These or other parties would be then sent back to bring up more stores from the advanced dumps, and in order that they might easily find the dump which contained the particular store, whether R.E., ration, or ammunition they required, the situation of each dump was marked by small flags of different colours. The whole scheme had been carefully worked out experimentally behind the lines by Major Locke, the D.A.Q.M.G. of the Division, and the proportion of each kind of store to be carried up by the carrying parties was arrived at after much discussion. To enable the Infantry to get out of their trenches and over the top instantly at the zero hour (the exact time laid down for the assault), about five hundred short ladders were required for the Brigade, and these had to be carried up to the trenches and distributed. About the same number of light wooden bridges were also constructed by the R.E., which were required to bridge our own lines of trenches to enable the Infantry in rear to advance on a wide front without a check. Major Acklom superintended the work of the distribution of the bridges and ladders.

Every night large batches of bridges and ladders were brought up to the reserve line by the transport wagons, and were then carried up into the trenches and hidden as much as possible out of sight of the Boche. The bridges were not placed actually in position over the trenches until as late as possible prior to the attack in order that they should not be observed and destroyed by the Boche, and when they were put up the wood-work was smeared over with mud to render them as inconspicuous as possible. In ordinary times of trench warfare it was, of course, unnecessary and very undesirable to crowd the supports and reserves close up behind the firing-line, and therefore the trenches of the troops in support were often half a mile in rear. When an assault, however, has to

ROAR OF A BOMBARDMENT

be delivered it is essential that the successive waves of the attacking force shall follow each other at very short distances apart, and in order to insure this it becomes necessary to assemble the waves in the forward area some little time previous to the attack. For this purpose it was, therefore, necessary to dig a number of "assembly" trenches for their use. These trenches were dug by each Battalion to meet its own requirements, and every advantage was taken of any existing old disused trenches which would with further excavation answer the purpose. It was only natural that the Boche should notice these new trenches and form his own conclusions as to their object. The result was that the work which was, of course, done at night was continually being interrupted by the enemy's fire, causing casualties to our working parties and damage to the trenches. However, the work was carried out in due course. In order to increase the density of the attacking force, it had been laid down that a few days prior to the attack a closing up of Brigades laterally should take place. Each was to close up to a shorter front. Our left was to remain as before, and our right was to move several hundred yards towards the left. The 101st Brigade were to take over the length of trench that we evacuated. This meant some little complication as regarded the digging of the assembly trenches, but all difficulties were got over by the combined efforts of the digging parties of both Brigades. It was, of course, extremely undesirable to crowd up the garrisons of the trenches any earlier than need be, as the denser the garrison of the area the heavier the casualties.

The enemy maintained a slow but methodical fire on our trenches, and the daily toll of officers and men, though not heavy, was continual. Trenches were often knocked in as soon as completed and had to be re-dug, but it was not until our great Artillery preliminary bombardment began on the morning of the 25th that we experienced the full intensity of the Boche reply. By this time the bulk of the work of carrying parties was over, but there was still necessarily a good deal of movement about the trenches by digging parties, ration parties, reliefs of front line garrisons, and individuals, some of whom could not fail to suffer from the increased enemy fire. Our trenches and communication trenches soon arrived at a stage when repairs were almost useless; it was impossible to keep up with the damage done. The dugouts did not entirely escape, and some of them were destroyed daily. It became a difficult physical feat to visit certain parts of the trenches. The weather became wet, and the top surface which fell in and blocked up the trenches became small hills of soft mud; it was no slight job to plough through these obstructions. At night getting about was easier because one was not confined to the communication trenches, but as the Boches swept the whole area with Artillery, and particularly with machine gun fire at frequent intervals, parties and individuals on the move at night had quite a lively time of it. Brigadiers and their headquarters were to move into their respective advanced headquarters on the day prior to the commencement of the Artillery bombardment, and we accordingly took up our abode in the newly constructed dugout off the new Usna and Tara reserve trench on the afternoon of the 24th June. The dugout was situated about fifty yards north of the Albert-Bapaume road, and contained three roughly hewn out underground chambers connected by tunnels. Each chamber had its own entrance shaft in the east or enemy's side of the reserve trench, from which steep steps led down to the room below; there was a solid roof of fifteen or twenty feet of chalk overhead, and upon the top of this was a mass of earth several feet thick, the result of the excavation of the trench and dugouts.

On the other side of the Bapaume road the

ROAR OF A BOMBARDMENT

headquarters of the 101st Brigade were housed in a similar dugout. There were numerous dugouts also running along more or less the whole length of the Tara-Usna trench for the accommodation of reserve troops. We utilised one of our rooms for an office and living accommodation for the staff, another as the clerk's room, and the third for the signallers. Telephones were installed so that we were in communication with Divisional Headquarters and with neighbouring Brigade Headquarters and our own units. The office room was about twenty feet by ten feet, the roof and the walls, about seven feet high, were strutted with baulks of timber, and a few planks nailed to posts served as a table. We each had our valises containing blankets and a change of clothes. The soldier servants had an adjacent dugout where the food was cooked. The floor and walls were very uneven, and, of course, the place was quite dark, which entailed the use of candles day and night stuck on to the baulks of timber on the walls. As a residence the place left much to be desired, but it was infinitely more comfortable than the average dugout occupied by Battalion and Company Headquarters, and at first it had the merit of being fairly dry. This, however, did not last, and after a day or two the water dripped freely from numerous cracks in the chalk overhead, and it was difficult to keep dry. I was fortunate in this respect, as my servant, Private Fraser, an old soldier, had dumped my bedding down in a corner which happened as it turned out to be the only spot which was not seriously dripped upon, but Major Soutry had particular bad luck, and the frequency of his sudden moves and the language used on each occasion in his efforts to find a dry spot became a standing joke to the other inhabitants of the dugout. Matters were not improved in this respect when the enemy took to shelling this trench line heavily, and a few very big shells dropped on to our roof. This treatment caused large excavations up above, which rapidly filled with rain water which quickly found its way down below.

Artillery of all calibre had for weeks past been concentrating in the Albert area, and by this time the numbers of batteries of field guns, howitzers, and heavy Artillery was enormous and in quite unprecedented numbers. The field Artillery batteries were planted more or less in line at slight intervals, about a thousand yards in rear of our Tara-Usna-Becourt line. The heavier Artillery was further back, and the big guns were in position west of the town. A French battery of the celebrated seventy-fives which was attached to the British troops took up its position a few hundred yards in rear of the Brigade Headquarters' dugout, and when it got to work its unceasing chatter day and night became monotonous. At 4 a.m. on the 25th the preliminary bombardment began with a roar which seemed to shake the earth. The air was split with the combined detonations of hundreds of guns of all calibres. From the trench outside one heard with the utmost satisfaction the rushing through the air of vast numbers of projectiles of all sizes flying over our heads on their way to the Boche lines. Inside the dugout, excepting for the bark of the French guns, only a confused roar was heard. This bombardment was to be maintained for five days. A very exact programme had been made out and issued to all concerned, so that one knew exactly what Artillery work was going on, what the rate of fire was, and the particular targets to be dealt with each day. Certain objectives in the Hun lines and in rear were to receive special treatment, and the concentrated bombardments one by one of places such at La Boisselle, Ovillers, Poizieres, Contalmaison, Martinpuich, etc., etc., each arranged for as a special item was a sight not to be forgotten. It was almost impossible to realise that any human being in any of these places could possibly survive.

ROAR OF A BOMBARDMENT

From a distance the place looked like the mouth of a volcano, but the clouds of ascending smoke and dust flickering with the flashes of bursting shells prevented any actual view of the scene beneath. It looked at the time as if no Boche could possibly remain alive in such an inferno, but unfortunately owing to the depths of their dugouts many did survive. An extremely important point was the blowing of gaps in the enemy's barbed wire entanglements prior to an assault by Infantry; unless this was properly done an advance would have had small chance of success, and so certain batteries were detailed for this duty only, and methodically carried out the work. Machine guns by night trained on the gaps prevented repairs being made. Daily reports were received from Battalion Commanders in the line as to the state of the enemy's wire and were passed on to Divisional Headquarters. While our bombardment was in progress we did not have it all our own way, as the enemy lost little time in replying in kind, and our trenches became very " unhealthy." The stretcher-bearers were kept busy, and when going round the trenches one constantly met wounded men, and the toll of the killed rapidly mounted up. One day on arriving at Lyle's Headquarters I found that a very big shell had crashed through into a deep dugout next door to his own, used by his Battalion signallers, all picked men, six of whom were killed instantly. This was a very serious loss to his Battalion, and Lyle was much cut up about it.

All the Battalions suffered more or less. The enemy maintained numbers of captive balloons for overlooking our lines, but our airmen soon destroyed the bulk of them, and the remainder were kept far behind. I happened to see two of them despatched. The balloon suddenly changed into a whiff of smoke and disappeared, a very satisfactory sight. I think it was on the third day of the bombardment that orders were received that the bombardment would be prolonged for an extra forty-eight hours, and that the "zero" hour—that is the exact moment at which the Infantry assault would be delivered—would be postponed accordingly. The attack was now to be at 7.30 a.m. on 1st July instead of at the same time on 29th June. This delay, which it was understood was due to some rearrangement of certain French Army plans, resulted in a modification of the Artillery programme, and the very apparent thinning down of the volume of the bombardment. The supplies of Artillery collected in the dumps was limited, and did not admit of the fire being maintained at the same rate for the longer period. The closing up of the Brigades on to a shorter front and the movements of the Battalions into the assembly trenches were matters which required a good deal of careful consideration and arrangement.

It was necessary that the troops should be in position without fail some little time at least before the zero hour, and, at the same time, owing to the violence of the enemy's fire the shorter time the troops were crowded up in the forward area the better. We had a final Brigade conference on the morning of the 30th June, which was attended by the commanding officers of units and the Brigade Staff. It had been necessary owing to the invaliding of Lieutenant-Colonel Dunbar-Stuart, who had hitherto commanded the 2nd Battalion, to find a successor to him, and Major Heniker, the second-in-command of the 1st Battalion, was accordingly placed in command of the 2nd Battalion. The " pow-wow " lasted a considerable time, and at its close General Williams unexpectedly arrived, just, as he said, to " Wish the Brigade good luck." That afternoon I visited the men in the front trenches and various company and Battalion Headquarters, and had a final chat with many old friends. Elphinstone, who I visited last, produced a whisky and soda, which I was most thankful to

ROAR OF A BOMBARDMENT

see. We drank success to the Brigade and the 3rd Battalion. All ranks were full of confidence. The Artillery bombardment had been so severe that judging by our losses under a very much lighter bombardment it was thought by many that the enemy would be too much demoralised to make much stand. Gaps had been successfully cut in the enemy's wire, our own wire had been removed from trenches in rear, and our front trench wire only required a few final cuts that night to get it out of the way. The ladders and the bridges were in position. Arrangements had been made for supplying the men with a good breakfast early the following morning, and at last, after weeks of arduous work, all was ready for " going over the top." In order to fill to some extent the gap which existed between the two right and the two left Battalions of the Brigade, a company of the 18th Pioneer Battalion was temporarily attached to the Brigade for the purpose of holding our front line opposite to La Boisselle. It was not intended that they should take an active part in the Infantry attack, but that the company should prevent any local advance on the part of the enemy from the village at this point.

CHAPTER XIII

THE MEMORABLE FIRST JULY

THE plan of attack, briefly, was that the 2nd Battalion should attack in columns of platoons on the right, and should be immediately supported by the 3rd Battalion following in the same order. The left attack was to be carried out by the 4th Battalion (on right) and 1st Battalion (on left) advancing almost side by side. The right and left attacks were to be each supported by a Battalion of the 103rd Tyneside Irish Brigade. During the night previous to the attack a couple of the Brigade trench mortars under Lieutenant E. F. Bowkett were to take up a position in No-Man's-Land, and open fire on and disorganise a certain trench in the defences of La Boisselle which it was considered would give trouble on the right flank of the 4th Battalion as that Battalion advanced. The 1st and 4th Battalions were to start at zero hour, but the 2nd and 3rd Battalions were to start two minutes later, owing to the necessity for allowing time for the debris to descend without hitting our men from the huge mine which was timed to go off under the enemy's front trench, opposite the 2nd Battalion, exactly at the zero hour. No-Man's-Land was here so much narrower than on the left where the other mine was. The machine gun company was posted on the slope of the ridge in suitable positions to cover the advance, and an elaborate Artillery barrage time-table had been worked out to cover the advance of the Infantry from one objective to another.

Maps had been issued, showing in different coloured chalks the various lines in the enemy's

THE MEMORABLE FIRST JULY 105

area, which at specified times were to be successively reached by the barrage. As it was impossible to obtain a view to the front from the trench in which the dugout was situated, just below the crest of the hill, the R.E. had constructed a small dugout to act as an observation station for my use in a trench a couple of hundred yards to the front on the further slope of the ridge, from which one theoretically could command a good view over No-Man's-Land and the Boche lines. This station was to be utilised by myself and by Brigadier-General Neville G. Cameron, commanding the 103rd Tyneside Irish Brigade, and was connected by telephone with my headquarters' dugout and with his headquarters, and so shortly before zero hour General Cameron and I repaired to this station. When we, however, got there we soon discovered that no satisfactory view to the front was really obtainable, and that if we wanted to see anything we should have to look over the parapet of the trench itself, when, by standing on the fire step, a view of the valley could be got. It was here that we waited for zero hour. Every watch had been synchronised the night before so that one knew to a few seconds the exact time. I had left Major Soutry at the headquarters, and had taken with me Captain Waller of the 2nd Battalion, who was then the Brigade Major's understudy.

As the watches marked the half-hour (7.30) the two huge mines on the flanks of La Boisselle simultaneously exploded with a concussion that shook the ground for miles round, and the attack began. The mine on the right had been charged with thirty tons of ammonal, and that on the left with twenty tons, so that the effect of the explosions was terrific. The bottom of the valley was quickly obliterated from our view by the dust thrown up and the smoke of countless shells, so that one could see little or nothing except the movements of the companies of the reserve Brigade as they went forward. They, too, were quickly lost to sight in the haze. After a time the dust cleared away to some extent, and it was possible to make out that apparently our men had effected an entry into the Boche trenches on the right, but it was impossible to form an opinion as to what was going on on the left. The enemy, in addition to maintaining a terrific fire on our troops as they advanced, did not overlook our back trenches in order to make it hot for any reserves who might be there, and the trench we occupied was from time to time swept by machine gun fire, and occasional bits of shell fell into it. While we were trying to make out what was going on, General Cameron was hit by a machine gun bullet in arm and thigh. We did what we could for him, and arranged for his removal by stretcher. A message was despatched at once by runner to the next senior officer of the 103rd Tyneside Irish Brigade, Lieutenant-Colonel G. R. V. Stewart, D.S.O., who was intercepted before his Battalion had left our trenches, and who, later on, arrived to take over temporary command of the Brigade.

As time went on and no news was forthcoming from the front I despatched runners to get into touch with our units. Some runners never came back, others did, and news was eventually collected which showed that while portions of the 2nd and 3rd Battalions had succeeded after enormous losses in capturing a short sector of the Hun trenches, there was only a remnant remaining of the 1st and 4th Battalions who had been almost annihilated while crossing the wide expanse of No-Man's-Land on our left. The general situation gradually became clear, and all news as received was telephoned to Divisional Headquarters, but the details could not be filled in immediately. That afternoon an officer sent back by Major Acklom, who was now in command of the remnants of the 2nd and 3rd Battalions, brought a report in reply to my inquiries stating that he was holding a length of

Our Ridge overlooking La Boisselle showing Large Crater.

THE MEMORABLE FIRST JULY 107

enemy front trench just north and south of the new big crater a hundred feet across, made by the explosion of the mine south of La Boisselle, and that he held also portions of the enemy support trench in front of him. Both his flanks were in the air, his men were much exhausted, he required a supply of bombs and water, and he recommended early relief by fresh troops. As regards the left it became evident that the attack had been pressed on with the most extraordinary heroism, but without avail. Officers and men had been literally mowed down, but in rapidly diminishing numbers they had resolutely pushed on to meet their deaths close to the enemy's wire. No-Man's-Land was reported to be heaped with dead. It was impossible to estimate at all accurately the extent of our losses, but steps were taken to ascertain from the advanced dressing stations the names of wounded officers and the numbers of the men dealt with.

It was not, however, until the next day that an approximate estimate of our casualties could be made, and even then much uncertainty existed as to the fate of individuals. Some time during the course of the morning I received orders to move forward the company of the 18th Pioneers as early as possible to attack La Boisselle itself, and orders were despatched to the officer commanding the company accordingly, but before the company could move fresh orders were to my relief received that it was to stand fast, and that two fresh Battalions from another Division would carry out the assault, and, finally, still further orders were received that instead of two Battalions two Brigades, the 57th and 58th, had been detailed for the purpose. The whole of the day and next night was taken up by receiving and issuing orders on a multitude of subjects and in dealing with a thousand matters which required adjusting, and the telephone was incessantly in use with the Divisional Staff. The enemy continued to maintain a very heavy fire on our trenches, and it was of little use to send runners across No-Man's-Land, which was swept by machine gun fire, except by using the mining tunnel which the engineers had constructed in connection with the big mine south of La Boisselle. This tunnel, in which it was impossible to stand upright, and was very narrow, lead from our front trench to the enemy trench which Major Acklom was holding, but it soon became congested with wounded and almost impassable, and communication by it was consequently extremely slow.

That night the situation was as far as could be ascertained as follows: On the right about a hundred and fifty officers and men of the 2nd Battalion, and about the same number of the 3rd under Major Acklom held the German trenches as described. The remainder of the two Battalions had been either killed or wounded. On the left the bulk of the 1st and 4th Battalions were lying dead in No-Man's-Land, and the remnants of these Battalions held a short length of our front trench north of La Boisselle. Of the 1st Battalion no officer at all, or even sergeant, could be found. Of the two Battalions of the 103rd Tyneside Irish Brigade in reserve a certain number were occupying parts of our trenches, and the company of the 18th Pioneer Battalion still remained in the line fronting La Boisselle. It was evident that the Brigade had practically been wiped out, and that it would be necessary to withdraw the remnants of it before long, and I received instructions that steps would be taken to relieve us as soon as possible. The 8th Division on our left had lost heavily, and had not succeeded in crossing No-Man's-Land, and were relieved by a fresh Division almost at once. It was said afterwards that the enemy expected our main attack to be directed against his trenches at La Boisselle and northward, and that he had not expected any serious attack southwards of that village, so that his preparations were made accordingly.

It is true that attacks at all points made that day

THE MEMORABLE FIRST JULY

along the whole line north of La Boisselle failed, and that a considerable advance was possible south of it, the further south the greater advance, but this may have been partly due to the greater width generally of No-Man's-Land to be crossed in the northern area. In our own case our men on the right had a comparatively narrow No-Man's-Land to get over, and just sufficient men survived the crossing to assault and capture the trenches, but on the left where No-Man's-Land was three times as wide, the time occupied in crossing under fire was three times as long, and the casualties were consequently so heavy that not a man survived to reach the opposite trench, much less a sufficient force to capture it. The fact that our men had made good and maintained their hold of the enemy's trenches south of La Boisselle was considered of enormous importance as it greatly facilitated the assault on the place by other troops who could use those trenches as a starting point for a flank attack on the village, and very shortly led to the fall of that stronghold.

The next morning I sent Major Soutry across to Major Acklom to get details of the situation, and impress upon him the absolute necessity of hanging on in his position at all costs until he was relieved, and to tell him that I was sending him supplies and such reinforcements as could be collected, and that the relief of his force would take place as early as it could possibly be managed. Major Soutry, after a difficult passage of the tunnel, returned in the afternoon and reported on the situation. On the 3rd inst. I got across to Major Acklom, and found his small force were holding, as had been reported, about three hundred yards of front trench and a short length of a support trench farther on. It appeared that the 2nd and 3rd Battalions had at first penetrated to some trenches several hundred yards beyond, but after severe fighting had been forced back by superior numbers to the trenches they now held. The officers and men were utterly tired out, having been without rest since the attack began, but they were in good spirits, and elated at their success. The enemy were still occupying the continuation of the trench on both flanks, and fighting was going on between bombing parties on both sides. Between Major Acklom's right and the nearest troops of the 101st Brigade a gap of many hundreds of yards existed, and the intervening trenches were occupied by the enemy so that both Major Acklom's flanks were in the air. There was little firing in No-Man's-Land at the time, and both going and coming I was able to cross in the open, which saved the slow progress of the tunnel, and I passed through successive lines of dead Tyneside Scots lying as regularly as if on parade.

The days and nights were so merged together and events happened so rapidly that it is impossible to remember the exact sequence of each. I was visited by, and had a long conference with, the Brigadier of the 58th Brigade, who had received orders to capture La Boisselle village, and he was good enough to send back a message later to say that he had followed the line of advance recommended with very small losses. The Commander of, I think, the 19th Division, whose Division was in reserve, was among the large number of officers coming and going at our Brigade Headquarters to get information of the situation. Colonel Mangles and other staff officers of our own Division paid us flying visits, brought orders, collected information, and departed. The telephone was never still. My own staff had no rest beyond an occasional short snatch of sleep at a time. Only a certain number of officers in each Battalion had been allowed to take part in the assault; any in excess of this number had been sent back to the transport lines some days previous to the attack. These officers were now sent for, and rejoined the fragments of their units. It was no time for sentiment,

THE MEMORABLE FIRST JULY

but apart from the feeling of personal loss of so many good friends it was apparent that we had sustained such a blow that the Brigade had almost ceased to exist, so in spite of the feeling of pride in the success achieved one worked with a constant sense of the altered conditions.

After the facts gradually became clear we found that out of the whole of the eighty officers of the Brigade who had gone over the top less than ten remained, the bulk of the remainder were killed and the rest wounded. Of the N.C.O.'s and men about eighty per cent were casualties. Nine hundred and forty all ranks were killed, and 1,500 odd were wounded. The 1st Battalion casualties included every officer and sergeant. In addition to the four commanding officers, Lieutenant-Colonels Elphinstone, Sillery, Lyle, and Major Heniker, who were killed, the list of officers killed included two of the seconds-in-command, and two of the adjutants and the remaining seconds-in-command and adjutants were wounded. No officers or men were taken prisoner. Our losses in killed were unnecessarily heavy owing to the fact that the Germans deliberately fired at and killed any wounded officer or man lying helpless in front of their trenches who made the slightest movement or showed any sign of life. Some officers and men waited until after dark and then managed with great difficulty to crawl towards our lines, and were assisted over the parapet by men who went over to meet them. Major Mackintosh, the second-in-command of the 4th Battalion, who was very severely wounded, was brought in under cover of darkness by his soldier servant, and Lieutenant E. Turnbull, of the 1st Battalion, who was knocked over when leading his platoon at the head of his Battalion, made his laborious way back to our lines at night in safety. The doctors in the advanced dressing stations had their hands full, and worked unceasingly by day and night.

There were many strange happenings which one

heard of later, and one of the strangest was the adventure of Lieutenant Dowse, the Brigade signalling officer. It had been laid down that when a certain line of enemy trench, called on our maps to the best of my recollection the Black line, had been captured, the various Brigade Headquarters were to move on and establish themselves in previously selected enemy dugouts used by the Huns as Battalion or Regimental Headquarters. The dugout in which our Brigade Headquarters was to be established was situated on the further outskirts of La Boisselle. Lieutenant Dowse, accompanied by two orderlies carrying telephones and material, was to move across as soon as our attacking force had captured La Boisselle, and pay out a wire as he went. He was to instal telephones in the new dugout, and open up communication as early as possible with our old headquarters. In his zeal, however, to get to work he started off a bit early, in fact as soon as he saw that our men on the right had got into the German front trench, he and his two orderlies walked calmly down the Bapaume road, and in the dust and smoke, actually did reach unnoticed by the enemy the dugout as arranged, which he found temporarily empty! At last, seeing no signs of our troops in the village, he thought it time to leave before the owners of the dugout returned, and having loaded himself and his two men with all sorts of booty from the German dugout, including some very special telephone instruments, which he removed from the walls and which greatly took his fancy, he set out on his return journey. Unfortunately, his party this time fell in with some Germans, and one of his men was killed, but he himself and the other orderly once more got across No-Man's-Land safely, and arrived at Brigade Headquarters with his strange assortment of German trophies, which he laid out on the table, and made his report of his experiences. Lieutenant E. F. Bowkett, with his two trench mortars in No-Man's-Land, had been heavily

THE MEMORABLE FIRST JULY

shelled as soon as he opened fire, and his mortars had been quickly smashed up, whereupon he took the survivors of his party and joined the troops attacking on the right, where he and they did most excellent service as a bombing party.

While the enemy's Artillery caused us heavy losses our casualties were mainly due to the intensity of the enemy's machine gun fire. In addition to the guns in the trenches many others were most cunningly placed in carefully hidden positions on the open slopes of " Sausage " and " Mash " valleys, north and south of La Boisselle. Not a sign showed the position of these guns; each was contained in a small shaft approached by an underground passage, and not a vestige of white chalk was allowed to appear on the surface to betray the position of the shafts; it had all been carefully removed underground. The top of the shaft was concealed by a covering of natural grass. These guns were never fired until the 1st July, and even aeroplanes had failed to detect their presence. Our Artillery bombardment had paid no particular attention to the open spaces, but had been devoted to the enemy trenches, batteries, and strong points, so that these unknown shafts escaped damage, and the guns were successfully brought into action at the moment of our assault. Orders were received that we were to be withdrawn on the 5th July, and arrangements were made accordingly. The remains of each Battalion as it came out in driblets from the trenches was collected together on the slope of the ridge between the Tara-Usna line and the town of Albert, and the Brigade marched through the town to the village of Mellencourt. The Tyneside Irish Brigade, who had also suffered severely, were withdrawn at the same time.

CHAPTER XIV

AT VIMY RIDGE

IT was understood that both Brigades were to be sent to a back area to re-organise, and that, in the meantime, two other Brigades would be temporarily attached to our Division. At Mellencourt we met the 110th Brigade, which belonged to the 37th Division, and we heard that this and another Brigade of the 37th Division were to be attached to the 34th Division, while we and the Tyneside Irish were to be attached to the 37th Division. This latter Division was holding a portion of the line to the north of Gommecourt. The next day we paraded for Sir W. Pulteney, the Corps Commander, who made us a very laudatory speech and emphasised the great importance tactically of the success attained. The whole Brigade when formed up now barely occupied the space of one Battalion, and the absence of so many old familiar faces made the occasion a sad one, but the men when asked the old tag if they felt downhearted roared out a stentorian " No." General Williams was present, and expressed his intense gratification with the splendid gallantry displayed, and hoped that we should soon rejoin his command. After a few days in Mellencourt, spent in re-organising the Battalions and other units as far as possible, the Brigade " embussed " for Pommier, the Brigade Headquarters proceeding by motor-car, and that evening I reported to Lord Edward Gleichen, commanding the 37th Division, whose Headquarters were established at Pas. He very kindly invited Major Soutry and myself to dinner, a most welcome meal. The Brigade was to be in reserve

AT VIMY RIDGE

and temporarily quartered at the village of Pommier, and after a few days' rest we were to take over a sector of the trenches a few miles away to the east. Lieutenant-General Sir T. D. O. Snow, K.C.B., commanding the corps of which the 37th Division formed a part, paid us a visit while we were at Pommier. Parties of officers and others were sent forward to familiarise themselves with the trenches, and all arrangements were made for relieving the present garrisons on a given night, but on the day on which the relief was to take place fresh orders were received to the effect that the 37th Division was to proceed to the Bruyer area behind the Vimy Ridge. The next day the Brigade marched north, and in the course of a few days we found ourselves at Divion, a small mining town a few miles south of Bruyer and about ten miles south of Bethune. The 103rd Tyneside Irish, now commanded by Brigadier-General Hubert E. Trevor, were quartered in the same area.

The strength of each of our Battalions was so greatly reduced that it was decided that as a temporary measure for tactical purposes the 1st and 4th Battalions should be amalgamated into one Battalion, and that the same arrangement should apply to the 2nd and 3rd, and a similar scheme was carried out in the 103rd Tyneside Irish Brigade. At Divion our men were naturally interested in the coal mines, and a good many made friends with the French miners, and some went down the shafts. For some time one found it difficult to realise the loss of all of our commanding officers and other officers with whom it had so often been a pleasure to discuss plans, and one missed them at every turn, but one had now to make a fresh start. During the time the Brigade was at Divion we were inspected by General Sir Charles Munroe, commanding the 1st Army, in which we now were serving. He was accompanied by H.R.H. Prince Arthur of Connaught, who was serving on his staff. The General, after the inspection, made a short but excellent speech, which was much appreciated by officers and men. It was now decided that the two Tyneside Brigades should take over a bit of the front trench, and that for this purpose they should be temporarily combined to act as one Brigade. Under these circumstances two Brigade commanders and staffs would not be required while the Brigades were serving in the trenches, and it was arranged that I, as the senior Brigadier, should command. The staff of the Tyneside Irish found ample employment in organising instructional classes in the back area. The bit of the trench which we were to take over was the Vimy Ridge section. It ran from the Souchez river on the north, southwards with a frontage of about a mile. The troops we were to relieve were a London Territorial Brigade, and the Brigade Headquarters was to be at Villers au Bois, five miles behind the lines. This had been a small village of substantially built houses, but at present one house only remained, and it was used as the Brigade Headquarters. The village was on high ground, which very gradually sloped downwards towards the east until the shallow Zouave valley was reached, and upon the farther side of the valley the celebrated Vimy Ridge rose abruptly to a height of about two hundred feet. At the northern end of the ridge, on our extreme left, there was a sudden drop to the Souchez river. Our front trench ran along the crest of the ridge opposite and parallel to the Boche trench, which was about forty or fifty yards distant. The central portion of our front trench was sufficiently advanced on the crest of the hill to admit of a support trench having been made a few yards behind it. On the right there was no room for a support trench, and the ground fell away abruptly behind the front trench. On the left the line was held by three or four wired-in grouse butts, detached posts, which could only be reached by night, as the approaches which were on the shoulder of the ridge were in view from the

AT VIMY RIDGE

Boche trenches on the low ground on our left front. As small mines were constantly being exploded by both sides the surface of the ground of No-Man's-Land was much broken up, and several fairly large craters existed.

The ground on the German side of the ridge sloped gently down, but no view except across the short No-Man's-Land on the crown of the ridge was obtainable from our trenches, though on our extreme left one had an extensive view over Lens and the mining district round it. To our north on the other side of the Souchez river rose the massif of Lorrette which was held by the troops of another Division, though some Batteries of the 37th Division were posted on the spurs of the south side of the hill near the village of Ablain. Souchez village, a heap of rubble, lay in the river valley to our left rear.

Behind it were Ablain and Carency, the remains of two villages. Very heavy fighting had occurred in this neighbourhood earlier in the war, and it was stated that in recapturing the Lorrette from the Germans the French casualties had exceeded 80,000. The point which struck me most about our position was that our hold on the extreme edge of the Vimy Ridge was undoubtedly very precarious, only a comparatively slight shove on the part of the enemy was required to push us over the edge, and as, in that case, no trench would have been tenable in the valley below, it would have been necessary to withdraw our front line to a trench about a mile to the rear. I suppose it was not worth while for the Hun, unless as part of a big advance, to make this push, for the reason that had he succeeded in shoving us off the ridge and occupied our trenches overlooking the Zouave valley, he would have left himself exposed to a flank fire from Lorrette. He already commanded a view from the top of the ridge into our lines almost as far back as Villers au Bois from a point called the " Pimple," a small pointed elevation on his side of No-Man's-Land on the extreme top of the ridge, so that unless he decided to advance in force elsewhere any permanent occupation of our front trench would have been of little use to him. There was always the possibility of an attempt being made to drive us off the ridge, and one had to always be prepared, but though small raiding parties frequently tried to rush our listening posts, no serious attack was made while we were there.

Captain H. W. Waller, who had returned to duty with the 2nd Battalion as a company commander, on one of these occasions greatly distinguished himself both by the excellence of his dispositions and by his own gallantry and initiative in a personal encounter which had disastrous results for the Hun. It was of immense importance to us to maintain our hold on the top of the ridge, even though we did only share the crown of it with the enemy, as in the case of our ever making an advance in force a jumping-off place on the ridge itself was of very great value. A considerable distance in the rear of the ridge a series of reserve trenches had been constructed, which extended back as far as the village of Carency. For defence purposes the front trenches were divided into right, centre, and left defences, one Battalion to each and one Battalion in reserve. The four Battalions (two Tyneside Scottish and two Tyneside Irish) took it in turns to form the reserve. The officers commanding Battalions were Major Acklom and Lieutenant-Colonel Porch, Tyneside Scottish, and Lieutenant-Colonel J. M. Prior and Major Fergusson, Tyneside Irish. Lieutenant Dowse and his section R.E. had been retained with the 34th Division, and we had been given temporarily a signalling section of the 37th Division under Lieutenant Griffiths, but otherwise the Brigade Staff was as before. Captain W. P. Kelly, an officer of the 3rd Battalion Tyneside Irish, had been acting as Brigade Intelligence Officer for some time past, and continued in that capacity.

AT VIMY RIDGE

The weather was fine but hot, and walking down to and round the trenches entailed a walk of about fifteen miles, including a climb up the ridge and a scramble among broken trenches on the top. So that to shorten it, Captain Kelly, who usually accompanied me, and I used to usually ride as far as Carency on our left and rejoin the horses at an exit from the reserve trench on the right. In this way much time and fatigue was saved. The top of the sides of the communication and reserve trenches were at this time bright with colour from the numerous wild flowers which grew in profusion, and when on our way back sandwiches and flasks were produced by my orderly, Private Johnstone, in some flower-bedecked trench, and we smoked and rested on a fire step for half an hour, it was hard to realise that the world was at war. Once we were disagreeably surprised while lunching in this way by the silly antics of a German plane, who swooped down for a moment or two and fired at us with a machine gun, but he made no hits. I am afraid that our efforts to obtain cover were more useful than dignified, but fortunately there was no audience.

The enemy's Artillery used to often harass the Zouave valley by a flanking fire from the left, and though this valley was quite out of his sight he knew that there was always a good deal going on there—men drawing water, or washing clothes, carrying parties taking rations and R.E. material forward, etc., etc. At the foot of the slope of the ridge were also dugouts for the tunnelling company and the various Battalion Headquarters, so that in the valley casualties occurred now and then from shell-fire. In front, fights between patrols and small raiding parties in No-Man's-Land and the explosions of small mines resulted in some loss, but on the whole our casualties while on the ridge were comparatively light. The O.C. tunnelling company, R.E., was continually devising methods for blowing up the Boche. He used to visit me

from time to time to report progress and arrange
for the explosion of a mine. On these occasions
a small party of Infantry were held in readiness
to rush out of our trench immediately after the
explosion, and occupy if possible the far side of
the newly formed crater, and kill and capture any
Boches who might be met with. Our tunnellers
had thrown out a protective gallery under No-
Man's-Land along our front, which acted as underground listening posts. Any tunnelling activity
on the part of the Boche was thus usually detected
in time to upset his plans. Our Corps Commander was now Lieutenant-General Sir Henry
Wilson, whose headquarters were at the château
of Ranchicourt, a few miles away from Villers au
Bois. The owner was a wealthy man who maintained the house during his absence as if he had
been living there, and the château itself was a
rather imposing-looking place standing in a small
well-wooded park. Sir Henry Wilson and three
or four members of his staff lived in the house; the
remainder messed in a large room in an adjacent
building which in the old days had been the
original château. The corps offices were in huts
erected in the park. I had the honour of dining
one night with the Corps Commander, and after
dinner a semi-official conference was held in the
library upon the subject of a possible future attack
by us on the Vimy Ridge and the numbers of
troops which would be required for the job. I was
interested to see, when the ridge was captured by
the Canadians in the following April, the estimate
I had ventured to give was in accord with the
numbers actually used. There was a parade on
one occasion in the park for the presentation of
Military Crosses to French officers by the acting
Army Commander, Lieutenant-General Haking.
The troops, after the presentation, marched past
the *décorés*, a French custom which has much to
recommend it.

CHAPTER XV

THE WORK OF RAIDING PARTIES

THE Brigade transport, which was encamped at villages behind Villers au Bois under Captain A. P. Ker, used to bring supplies of all kinds up to the lines nightly and dumped them on the Carency-Souchez road, near the ruins of Souchez village, from whence carrying parties took the stores forward. It was a long job for the transport, and a midnight meal of some kind was desirable on the return journey. A soup kitchen was therefore arranged by Captain Marrs in one of the broken-down houses of Carency, where hot pea-soup and biscuits could be obtained free by any soldier at any time during the night. There was a Battery of our guns hidden in the wreckage of the houses and gardens of the village, and the gunners were glad to avail themselves of the use of this kitchen, and were welcome guests. The soup kitchen was under the charge of a couple of our oldest men, who ran it very well. Carency was shelled at intervals, so that the job was not altogether a sinecure. When we returned to Armentieres we established in the village of Chappelle d'Armentieres a similar soup kitchen, and found a ruined shop in the main street which answered the purpose admirably. It had a real counter, over which the soup and biscuits were handed out to applicants in the most approved style. A bench or two were knocked up, and the men could sit down and eat in some comfort. On cold nights the kitchen was much used by the transport men and by carrying parties returning from the trenches, and though so many and more important events have since that time occurred to blunt their memory of trifles, I dare say the soup kitchen may yet remain not unpleasantly in the recollections of some of those who visited it.

When the order came after we had been five weeks in occupation of the ridge for the two Brigades to move up to Armentieres I was not altogether sorry. The Brigades were on the most cordial terms, and worked together without the slightest hitch, and one was sorry that the combination should come to an end, but neither of them was really more than a very disorganised remnant of its original self, and the two combined only numbered about half the strength of a Brigade. The responsibility, therefore, of holding the ridge with so small a force was not under the circumstances one which anyone would wish to retain longer than necessary, and it was with a distinct feeling of relief that one saw our successors arrive and we once more started off for Armentieres. In the meantime the 34th Division had suffered a grievous loss in the death of their gallant Commander, Major-General C. Ingouville-Williams, who was killed at Mamitz Wood, on the Somme, on the 22nd day of July, 1916. It is not too much to say that his death was a serious blow, not only to his Division, but to the Army in France. Extremely active in mind and body, restlessly keen and full of energy, a thoroughly practical soldier of great experience in France, he had a personal charm of his own and a generous disposition, which, in spite of a hot temper, gained for him the admiration and affection of his subordinates. He fell a victim of his own reckless courage in carrying out a self-imposed duty in the ranks of another Division. The funeral, which I attended, was on a very imposing scale, appropriate to the high military rank of the deceased General, and was attended by a very large number of Generals and other officers, and it was evident from their remarks that it was generally recognised that

WORK OF RAIDING PARTIES

the Army had lost a leader who could ill be spared and who would undoubtedly have risen to much higher rank.

While the Brigade had been in reserve at Divion I had paid occasional visits to Bethune, which was a charming old country town, its market square surrounded by fine old tall quaintly gabled houses, centuries old, and in its centre an ancient Town Hall and tower. There were practically no troops in the town, and of course this was exactly the Boche idea of a suitable target for his Artillery. The town, however, lay about nine miles behind the fighting line, and was, therefore, out of range of any but heavy guns, so one fine market day, when the market, as the Hun well knew, would be in full swing and the market place crowded, he turned on his twelve-inch guns with the Town Hall as his mark. He succeeded in killing a number of inoffensive women and children, some old men, and two or three soldiers, and in creating some huge craters in the square, and what no doubt delighted him as much almost as the murder of civilians did, he reduced the picturesque old buildings round the square to ruins. I went over to see the damage a few days later, and I heard afterwards from an officer who accompanied his Majesty that King George had visited the place the day after the Boche bombardment, which they fortunately had not repeated. It was such senseless acts as the murder of civilians, the unnecessary destruction of property, and last but not least the killing of our wounded in cold blood, that gradually created in our ranks a deep and lasting hatred and disgust of the Hun. As has been said, " He was a brute and remains a brute," and I am happy to think that the Tyneside Scottish Brigade should have been instrumental in ridding the world of an appreciable number of these human vermin.

The march back to Armentieres was without any particular incident, and we soon found ourselves holding the same section of the trenches as before, except that the left of our line was extended across the Armentieres-Lille road, to a distance of about three hundred yards to the north. We held on the left of this road a detached block of buildings which had been a factory of some kind, which formed a strong point about five hundred yards in rear of our front trench. We were now attached to the 2nd Anzac Corps, under the command of Lieutenant-General Sir Alexander Godley, whose headquarters were at Bailleux, nine miles in the rear. The Tyneside Irish Brigade had resumed its separate existence immediately we left the trenches on Vimy Ridge, and were also quartered at Armentieres, but very soon were sent back to the Somme. The re-organisation of our Brigade was now pushed on, and officers and men were sent to us from a variety of units to bring us up to strength. At first very few of our own wounded returned to us, and I got letters from men complaining that they had, on recovering from their wounds, been posted to units in which they were entire strangers. As one corporal, who had been posted to a south country Battalion, wrote, " They don't understand what I say, and I can't understand them." I tried hard to get our own men back, and was fortunate enough to enlist the sympathies of the 2nd Army Commander, Sir Herbert Plumer, with the result that a certain number of our men did eventually return to us, but in nearly every case the man, to his annoyance, was posted to the wrong Battalion, not the one in which he and his friends had enlisted and with which he had home associations. This I remedied by transferring the men to their own units, until orders were received from the Adjutant-General's branch at General Headquarters that this could not be permitted. In order to comply with this order and at the same time to fall in with the very natural wish of the men to serve with their old friends, I " retransferred " the men to the wrong unit and " attached " them only to their old one. This

WORK OF RAIDING PARTIES

also was vetoed by General Headquarters on the grounds that the clerical work of records would be unnecessarily complicated.

While it was quite evident that the number of men in the Tyneside Scottish Depot, from whom we could draw our reinforcements, was very limited and we could not possibly expect to regain our full strength without the accession of a very large number of men from elsewhere, there seemed to be no reason for sending our wounded men to join other units, or for posting men to Battalions in the Brigade other than their own. Esprit de corps and the content of the soldier are such valuable assets that I cannot help thinking that the human element was too much overlooked in dealing with this question. As a Brigade we soon began to revive. Commanding officers were appointed. Lieutenant-Colonel F. A. Farquhar, Royal Scots, was appointed to the command of the 1st Battalion, Lieutenant-Colonel P. B. Norris to the 2nd Battalion, Major S. Acklom, D.S.O., M.C., was promoted to Lieutenant-Colonel to command the 3rd Battalion, and Lieutenant-Colonel C. P. Porch, second-in-command, 18th Pioneers, to the 4th Battalion. Vacancies among the company officers were filled up, and the Battalions gradually approached their full establishment. Finding that a certain large detached house formerly used by the Divisional Artillery was available, I arranged that we should use it as Brigade Headquarters. The house stood by itself in a garden a few hundred yards in advance of the southern extremity of the town on a road leading down to the trenches, and the accommodation was suitable. Here we lived off and on for months undisturbed by the Boche. This strange immunity from the attentions of the Boche was said to be attributable to the fact that the house belonged to an influential German, and that it was spared accordingly. I don't know if this statement was true, but whatever the reason was, while we were there no shell ever fell within several hundred yards of us, though many went over our heads.

We soon found that the Boche Artillery was very much more aggressive than when we were formerly in the area, and that he had developed a new and very large species of " oil can," a thing shaped like a cylinder and weighing a hundred pounds, which when dropped into our trenches instantly obliterated the parapets and shelters for many yards and left deep craters instead. These " oil cans " were thrown by a trench mortar with a range of a thousand yards, and sometimes were seen in flight, in which case there was a chance of getting out of the way. Parts of our line suffered very severely from these " oil cans "; as soon as a destroyed length of parapet had been laboriously rebuilt by a night's toil, it would be again destroyed. This was particularly the case with a section of front trench some hundred yards to the right of the Lille road, where the casualties were heavy. The Boche, however, by no means had it all his own way, as our trench mortars had much improved by this time, and the larger size manned by Artillery crews could throw a bomb weighing sixty pounds a distance of six hundred to eight hundred yards. These bombs were spherical with a rod attached about a foot long, which fitted into the barrel of the mortar. They did tremendous damage to the Boche trenches, and when we had a combined straf of several of these mortars, plus some of our smaller ones, the result from our point of view was most gratifying. I recollect on one occasion while watching a straf, seeing among the planks and other debris blown into the air the body of a Boche who was shot up thirty or forty feet; I don't suppose he worried us any more. The enemy frequently shelled the town of Armentieres, as well as Chappelle d'Armentieres, our gun positions, and of course our trenches. On one occasion he managed to explode an Artillery dump

WORK OF RAIDING PARTIES

in our lines with disastrous results, and on another he discovered at last the whereabouts of one of our Batteries which was hidden in a row of houses, of which the fronts on the ground floors had been removed and camouflaged by canvas painted to look like brick-work. The Divisional Artillery in the area was under the command of Lieutenant-Colonel Wilberforce and the co-operation of the Artillery and the Brigade was most cordial. Many an Artillery straf was arranged at our Brigade Headquarters, but even more interesting were the conferences which took place about once a week on the planning of raids on the enemy's trenches. These raids required the most careful preparation and the closest attention to minute detail. The planning of each raid affected the Artillery, Infantry, trench mortar batteries, and machine gun company in the Brigade area. The transport also were interested, and neighbouring Brigades had to be informed, and usually the assistance of the Corps Artillery was invoked to bring fire from heavy guns and howitzers on to certain points in the enemy's lines while the raid was in progress.

In order that the enemy should not get accustomed to any particular form of raid, variety in method was necessary. Some raids were carried out by small parties, others by much larger ones. Sometimes a raid would be made on a front trench only, sometimes both the front and support trench would be raided. The times for raids had to vary as well as the particular bit of trench to be raided, but all our raids took place after dark. Too full a moon was a disadvantage, and a dark windy night with the wind blowing from the Boche lines to ours was very suitable. Having decided upon which piece of enemy trench the raid should take place, a plan of it was marked out by a deep furrow on a piece of open ground half-way back towards Erquinghem. This plan was full size, and showed the front, support, communication trenches, and dugouts. The size of the raiding party varied according to the scheme, from two officers and twenty men to half a Battalion, and it was essential that every officer and man taking part should be thoroughly familiarised with the geography of the trenches to be raided, and with his own particular rôle in the raid. For this reason each raiding party carefully rehearsed the raid on the dummy trenches several times prior to the actual raid until everyone became part perfect. Small raiding parties usually entered the enemy's trench at one point, turned to right and left, killed or captured any Boches they met, did as much damage as they could in the time laid down, perhaps ten minutes, and got back to our trench as quickly as possible.

Larger raiding parties were split up into several groups, each of which had its own particular and clearly defined job. Entry into the enemy's trench would be affected at two or three different points. It would be the duty of some parties to push on up particular communication trenches a certain specific distance, or to raid a limited piece of the support trench. Other parties would be detailed to meanwhile clean up the front trench of any Boches hiding in dugouts. " Stops " would have to be placed at the ends of any piece of trench raided to prevent parties of the enemy crawling up on the flanks of the raiders and perhaps cutting off their retreat. In order to render a raiding party as invisible as possible and to prevent its detection in No-Man's-Land prior to the assault, the precaution was always taken of blacking the faces and hands of the raiders, and to allow of men being recognised as friends on their return journey the collar of each man's tunic was lined with white material which did not show when usually worn, but could clearly be seen when the collar was raised and the white lining was exposed. It was very important that some such distinguishing sign should be adopted to prevent parties and individuals being fired on in error after a raid by

WORK OF RAIDING PARTIES

our men in the front trench, and this arrangement was found, after trials of various other devices, to be the best. Before any raid could be carried out it was very necessary that gaps should be cut in the enemy's wire at suitable places, and also in a good many other places, in order to deceive the Boches as to our intentions. The gap cutting was as a rule done by Artillery and trench mortars. The Artillery, during a raid, co-operated by maintaining a heavy fire for a few moments on the trench to be attacked, and then on to rear trenches and points on the flanks, in order to prevent the Boche from bringing up reinforcements. The machine gun company maintained a fire on certain selected points.

We used to get the Corps Artillery to co-operate, and it was pleasant to hear their heavy projectiles lumbering along overhead, but no doubt the Boche at the other end of the journey had his own opinion. The zero hour fixed for a raid, i.e., the actual moment when the raid was to begin, always varied; sometimes the raid took place soon after it was dark, but any time during the night up to an hour before dawn would do. We never carried out a raid by day, though this was done occasionally elsewhere. A fairly wide No-Man's-Land was, generally speaking, desirable for raid purposes, as it facilitated the cutting of the wire. Where No-Man's-Land was very narrow there was always a chance of damage being done to our own wire and trenches by our own wire cutting guns. For this reason we never could do a raid at one particular part of our line at Armentieres, known as the Rue de Bois salient. Here our wire and the Boche wire was separated only by a few yards. When the width of No-Man's-Land permitted it, a raiding party would beforehand silently emerge from our own trenches, and would lie down as near as possible to the enemy's trench without alarming his sentries. There was always the risk of an enemy's patrol stumbling on to the party in the dark, but that could not be avoided. While the party was quietly moving to its place in No-Man's-Land our display of Very lights in that particular section of the line had to be very limited, but a total cessation of lights was undesirable, as it might have aroused the suspicions of the Boches. Exactly at zero hour the Artillery opened fire and the raiding parties rushed forward, each party to carry out its own particular task.

CHAPTER XVI

SPIES IN THE BRITISH LINES

No-Man's-Land instantly blazed with Boche lights and the flashes of bursting shells, and the incessant roar of the guns had a very theatrical effect. At the end of the arranged period, usually fifteen minutes, the signal for the retirement of the raiding parties would be given by a special rocket signal fired from our front trench, and by the blowing of whistles in the Boche trenches. Upon the signal being given each party withdrew as quickly as possible from the Boche lines, avoiding the enemy fire in No-Man's-Land by moving to a flank and not straight across, bringing with them the prisoners and booty which had been captured. On one occasion a very truculent prisoner was being hustled, fighting and kicking, across No-Man's-Land, and an officer with the party noticed that it might be impossible, time being pressing, to get him over alive. He knew that live prisoners, capable of giving information, were particularly required just then, so he said to the men bringing the prisoner in, "Try coaxing," whereupon one of our men, a bit of a wag, called out in "a-call-the-dog-voice," "Come along, Fritzy, old boy, come along, good old Fritz, you shall have such a good dinner." At the word "dinner" the struggle instantly ceased, and the Hun walked in like a lamb amid the roars of laughter of his captors. Our wounded were taken back from the enemy's trenches to our lines immediately the casualties occurred so as to obviate the risk of a wounded man being left to the mercy of the Hun. The Artillery continued to maintain fire on the enemy's trenches for some time after the recall signal, in order to prevent the enemy from interfering with our withdrawal, and to thus give more time to get back to any of our men who might be hit on the return journey, and to those who had lost their way. After a raid a roll call took place, and the names of the missing were noted. As a rule missing officers and men could be accounted for, they had been seen to fall, but in some cases no evidence would be forthcoming, and the fate of the missing man was sometimes never known. A raiding party was always formed of volunteers, of whom there was no end.

A raid required not only extreme bravery on the part of the men, but also heroic qualities on the part of the leaders. They had to have, moreover, the entire confidence of the men behind them. These qualities were most pronounced among the young officers of the Tyneside Scottish, who, mere boys as many of them were, gained a splendid reputation for themselves, remarkable even in those days of heroic deeds performed daily on every side. Many of the bravest officers and men lost their lives, others were wounded, and some were missing. The uncertainty of the fate of the latter was always a matter of great concern to commanding officers and myself; to be killed outright was a clear cut and definite end, but to be missing might, and probably did, mean to be lying wounded in No-Man's-Land, and being frozen to death in the bitterly cold night. After a raid patrols were invariably sent out as soon as possible to search for, and, if possible, recover any missing officer and man, but the Boche did his best to make this a very difficult matter. The raids usually produced German prisoners, who often provided useful information to the Intelligence Department. As soon as the results of a raid were reported by telephone, inquisitors in the shape of Intelligence officers were sent by the corps to Brigade Headquarters to interrogate the Huns, and extract out of them any information they had to give. This

SPIES IN THE BRITISH LINES 133

process sometimes took several hours, and it often entailed an all night sitting. So many officers and men distinguished themselves in their raids in which we as a Brigade specialised, that it is impossible to recall here any but a few of their names, but the large number of Military Crosses, D.C.M.'s and M.M.'s that were awarded at that time, showed how the work done was appreciated by the Higher Authorities. Among those to greatly distinguish themselves was Captain C. H. Daggett of the 4th Battalion which, when he fell leading the last of a series of raids in which he had taken part, lost a very gallant and devoted officer.

And there was Lieutenant W. Algie who, when in command of a small party that was intended, and had been trained at rehearsals to act as a reserve in the enemy's front trenches, finding that the leading party had been destroyed outside the enemy's wire, and that the success of the raid was in danger, instantly on his own initiative transformed his party into the leading one, rushed it up the enemy's communication into the support trench, and while there shot nine Germans with his own hand. This young officer was recommended for the V.C., but was awarded the D.S.O. One of our most ambitious and successful raids was that carried out by half the 4th Battalion under the personal command of Lieutenant-Colonel Porch. The raid resulted in a large number of Huns being killed and much damage to enemy's trenches, and also a satisfactory capture of Boche prisoners. After each successful raid we received telegrams of congratulation from the Army Commander and Corps and Divisional Commanders which were much appreciated. Lists of the names of officers and men who had especially distinguished themselves were submitted to Army Headquarters for favourable consideration for " Immediate Reward," and in a few days' time the Brigade was the richer by the honours awarded.

The "Immediate Reward" system for acts of gallantry was a novelty, and is undoubtedly a very great improvement on the old system, which often entailed so long a wait as to almost disconnect the award with the deed which won it. Among the recipients of the Military Cross was the Rev. J. MacHardy, the Roman Catholic Chaplain attached to the Brigade, whose pleasure it was to share with the men the hardships and dangers of life in the front trenches, and who gained the respect of officers and men of all denominations. The Division was now to lose the services of Lieutenant-Colonel Mangles, the senior general staff officer, who received an appointment at the War Office, and his departure was much regretted by all of us who had the pleasure of working with him. He was succeeded by Lieutenant-Colonel Brain. When Major-General Ingouville-Williams was killed Brigadier-General C. L. Nicholson was appointed to command the Division with the temporary rank of Major-General. It was a strange coincidence that like his predecessor he should have been promoted from the command of General William's Brigade, the 15th. Lieutenant-Colonel Chant had for some months been the assistant Adjutant and Quartermaster-General. We had been for some little time at Armentieres before the rest of the 34th Division returned. Divisional Headquarters were then established at Crois de Bac, three or four miles west of Armentieres. We were still under the command of Lieutenant-General Sir Alexander Godley, the 2nd Anzac Corps Commander, who very often came to see us, and took much more than the usual official interest in the Brigade. I sometimes enjoyed his hospitality at his headquarters at Bailleul. His A.D.C. was a marvel at producing good dinners, which one fully appreciated after our somewhat rough and ready fare at Brigade Headquarters.

We all knew that in spite of all precautions Boche spies and agents abounded behind our lines, and

SPIES IN THE BRITISH LINES 135

that they were able to communicate much useful information to the enemy, so that the greatest care was taken to prevent news of any prospective raid being spread about. Officers and men were enjoined to say nothing to anyone, and were, during training, quartered behind the lines as a separate unit. But the Boche was very persistent, and on one occasion, at least, his spy from his sheer effrontery, coolness, and courage deserved to get away with the news. There was a Brigade, who shall be nameless, who held the section of trenches on our left, that was about three hundred yards north of the Lille road. On their front was at one point an enemy salient which reduced the width of No-Man's-Land to about seventy yards. There had been a great deal of talk of the numbers of men who were, it was said, unnecessarily employed by units in the line on sentry duty in the trenches, and the Brigade in question being much under establishment it was decided to abolish a number of possibly superfluous sentry posts, including those hitherto maintained at the entrances of certain communication trenches and at the junction of these trenches with the reserve and support lines. Well, one day a typical French peasant, with a spade over his shoulder, was seen to slouch along the main road from Armentieres towards the trenches. There was nothing unusual in this, as the peasants were in the habit of working in the fields close up to the reserve trench, and were indeed often under shell fire while ploughing their land. This man, therefore, attracted no particular attention. It appeared later that he walked some distance up a side road and entered a communication trench, from which he made his way into a support trench. While he was passing along on his way to the front trench he was noticed by some men who were engaged on a job a short way off, which entailed their temporarily laying aside their rifles. They shouted to him, and he then ran, and emerged into the front trench exactly opposite the narrow bit of No-Man's-Land referred to, scrambled up the parapet of an unoccupied bay, through some broken wire, and rushed doubled up across to the Boche trenches, where he disappeared. He was evidently expected as the enemy did not fire at him. A couple of men in the front trench in an adjacent bay stated that they fired at and thought they hit the man as he ran across No-Man's-Land, but this was merely conjecture. This spy certainly took over to the Hun valuable information as to local matters, such as the position of our guns and dumps, the disposition and strength of our units, and many other details which would be of great utility to the enemy, and he probably was able to give news of other and more important matters not of a local character.

As our Brigade, though it had received certain drafts, was still very much under establishment the question of the possible reduction of the numbers of trench sentries had received attention, and certain small reductions had been made, but after this event it was evident that there was a limit to the reduction which could be safely made. The incident, as was to be expected, caused a good deal of stir at the time locally, and one breathed a selfish sigh of relief that the occurrence had not happened in our lines. Some time after we returned to Armentieres we lost, to our great regret, the services of Major Soutry, who was promoted to the General Staff of a Division; he was replaced as Brigade Major by Major F. G. Troubridge, who had formerly belonged to the 1st Battalion Tyneside Scottish, but had latterly been serving on the 34th Divisional Staff. The Brigade also suffered another loss in Captain W. P. Kelly, whose services were urgently required to take up the appointment of second-in-command of his Battalion in the Tyneside Irish. He had done a great deal of valuable work as Brigade Intelligence Officer, and had also proved himself an excellent Mess President. He was always a cheery and pleasant companion,

SPIES IN THE BRITISH LINES

and his death from wounds, very shortly after he left us, was deeply regretted by us all. The officer appointed to succeed him as Brigade Intelligence Officer was Lieutenant P. H. L. Brough, also from a Battalion of the Tyneside Irish.

The continual strain of service with the trench mortar battery existence had at last told on Lieutenant E. F. Bowkett, who had been only able to hang on to his job by sheer determination until at last he had to be invalided, and his place was taken by Lieutenant C. N. Levin from one of our own Battalions, who proved himself a most capable successor. The changes among the officers of the Battalion owing to casualties was unceasing, and it became very difficult to know even the names of many of them. Commanding officers found a similar difficulty they told me, but we were always lucky, and the quality was maintained. This trench warfare was very largely an affair of platoon commanders, and the reputation of their Battalion and the Brigade was to a great extent in their hands, and safely so. Our Army Commander, Sir Herbert Plumer, paid several visits to Brigade Headquarters while we were in the trenches, and one day he did us the honour of lunching with us informally. He was accompanied only by one of his A.D.C.'s, and I am afraid that being unprepared for the lunch portion of the visit we provided most meagre fare. During the visit of H.R.H. the Duke of Connaught to the troops in France he spent a day or two in the area of the 2nd Army, and, in the company of General Sir Herbert Plumer, visited the front trenches at Ypres and other places, and stayed a few hours at Bailleul. Some of our officers and men who had distinguished themselves were presented to H.R.H. at a small function arranged by Sir Alexander Godley at Corps Headquarters. Every now and then an aerial fight took place over our heads between considerable numbers of planes on both sides, and occasionally a machine was brought down in our lines. One dark night, about 11 o'clock, the noise of an aeroplane was heard flying up from the trenches very low over our headquarters, and the roar of the engine was so loud, it seemed to almost graze the roof as it passed over. After a few minutes it came back from the direction of the town and did the same thing. A third time this very mysterious plane came just over our roof on its way back from the trenches, and followed the road back to Armentieres. We speculated as to the possible meaning of this manœuvre, but the problem was not solved until the next day when we were informed by the Division to whom a report had been made in due course the night before, that the machine had landed in a field five miles or so behind the lines, and had been seen by a party of a labour Battalion close by. The two German officers had alighted, and were surprised to find themselves the prisoners of a party armed with spades, who had quickly surrounded them. The Germans explained that they had lost their way, and had flown up and down from the Boche lines to ours, using the road as a guide, and had not been able to make up their minds which was their own side. Eventually they had chosen the wrong one.

CHAPTER XVII

THE RIGOURS OF WINTER

THE question of providing greater security from shell-fire for our officers and men in the trenches was one which was receiving a great deal of attention, and it was decided that a certain number of concrete dugouts should be constructed which would be practically proof against ordinary shell-fire. The construction of these was planned and carried out under the supervision of the R.E., and entailed heavy work on Infantry carrying parties. Before we left this part of the line a few had been completed, and others were under construction. To prevent unnecessary casualties in case a shelter should be hit, there was a standing order in force that at no time should more than two or three officers congregate in a shelter at one time, and the same applied to the concrete dugouts; but perhaps the order was not so understood, for a party of young officers had on one occasion unwisely met together in one of the newly constructed concrete dugouts in the support trench, and a shell, penetrating into the interior, had resulted in several being killed and others wounded, a serious loss to the Battalion concerned. The fact was that unless a prohibitive quantity of material were used it was impossible to erect an absolutely shell-proof dugout on or half below the surface of the ground, and deep digging was impossible in this area owing to water. No doubt the Boche suffered to some extent from the same difficulties, which was some consolation.

Under Lieutenant-Colonel Norris' auspices the 2nd Battalion about this time burst out into a theatrical troop called the "Yellow Diamonds," which quickly made a name for itself, and attracted big audiences. The stage-manager was Lieutenant C. H. Crabbe, who had had considerable experience on the stage at home. Two of the stars were Captain A. W. McCluskey, M.C., the Adjutant of the Battalion, and Lance-Corporal Charles, who took female parts most successfully. It was not long before the manager of the Divisional troop, "The Chequers," on the look-out for talent, cast an envious eye on members of the "Yellow Diamonds," and some of them were induced to join "The Chequers." These entertainments, which were held when the Brigade was in reserve at Erquinghem, in a good sized hall in the town, were very popular with all ranks. For an hour or two men could forget that such people as Huns existed, though it was necessary to take precaution to prevent any ray of light escaping from the hall, or an unpleasant reminder to the contrary might have been forthcoming.

In each corps area behind the lines was a caravan fitted up as a home for carrier pigeons, and each Brigade was supplied with birds which were in charge of its pigeon men. Fresh birds were taken down the front line daily. Birds were only kept in the trenches for twenty-four hours, and were then released. The Germans had a similar arrangement, and birds were often targets of a fusillade, but were very seldom hit. The pigeon men in the trenches had orders when releasing a bird at the end of its twenty-four hours to invariably attach a dummy message to its leg for practice sake. The sense of the message did not much matter; the messages were intended for the edification only of the "pigeoneer" at the home, so that these dummy messages generally merely expressed the views of the sender on the situation in general and his own in particular in somewhat unorthodox language. "Fed-up," with adjectives, was a term much in use.

THE RIGOURS OF WINTER

During a spell in reserve at Erquinghem orders were received that the Brigade and some other troops in the neighbourhood would be inspected by the Commander-in-Chief, Sir Douglas Haig, and one wet morning found us drawn up in line along the main road of the place. Drafts had been gradually filling our ranks, and we were now nearly up to establishment. The men looked uncommonly well on parade, clean and tidy, and when the C.-in-C. rode along the front he expressed his pleasure at the very smart and soldierly appearance they presented. He was accompanied by a staff officer and an A.D.C., and was followed by a couple of mounted orderlies, one of whom carried a small Union Jack mounted on a lance. The Corps Commander, Sir Alexander Godley, and, of course, the Divisional Staff were present. Other troops were formed up in continuation of our line, and after the parade the whole Brigade marched past the C.-in-C., who took up his position on one side of the road. As the Brigade was returning to its area by a roundabout way we met a Battalion of Colonial troops who were to have been inspected and who had lost their way. The language the C.O. used no doubt was a relief to his feelings.

While we were in the trenches we had a visit from some of our Tyneside Committee. The party included the chairman, Colonel Sir Thomas Oliver, Colonel Sir Charles Parsons (who was Honorary Colonel of one of the Tyneside Irish Battalions), Colonel Joseph Reed, Colonel Joseph Cowen, and Colonel Sir Johnstone Wallace. In order to avoid as far as possible any repetition of the discomforts which they had suffered at Fleurbaix, we this time arranged that rooms in a well-furnished house in Armentieres should be engaged for them, and that they should sleep there and take their meals at our Headquarters. Our visitors were most welcome, and brought with them a breath of fresh air from England. We heard of all sorts of interesting happenings which were not in the papers, and which probably the censor would have banned, and our talks on both the evenings they were with us lasted long in the night. As one always slept in one's clothes late hours made little difference to us. The visit was to have brought us, we heard, a present of a consignment of fish which our guests had laid in at Boulogne, but unfortunately the parcel had been mislaid. It was a regrettable incident, fish were rare, and we wondered who had had the benefit of the gift, until a fortnight later a member of the mess, noticing a strange but particularly unenticing odour in the room in which his blankets were spread, at last made an investigation, and came across, hidden under a pile of odds and ends, the large parcel of our long lost fish. How it got there was a never-explained mystery. A suitable spot in the ruined garden close to a half-buried unexploded bomb dropped one night by a Boche plane marks the last piscatorial resting-place.

One of the many remarkable inventions of the war was the instrument which indicated the position of hidden enemy's guns by means of sound. A special branch was set up whose duty it was to find out and record the exact position of enemy's heavy batteries firing at long ranges, whose whereabouts could not be otherwise accurately located. The working of the instrument is beyond my knowledge, but the information thus afforded to our gunners and airmen was most valuable, and led to the destruction of many a Boche Battery. Whether the Germans were eventually similarly equipped I don't know, but, generally speaking, it was merely a matter of time for them to become acquainted with the inventions of the allies and to adopt something similar. At the beginning of the war their instruments of all kinds were very highly finished articles, but as the effects of the Blockade gradually became more and more felt, substitutes became necessary, and workmanship and finish

THE RIGOURS OF WINTER 143

deteriorated. While the clothes worn by their men captured in action were always good, their bread ration was extraordinarily unappetising, a hard brick of a blackish colour with a very unpleasant flavour.

Though the ranks were now almost full once more there was an almost complete absence of pipers, nearly the whole of them having met their deaths on 1st July when playing their companies over the top. The large majority of the pipes had also disappeared. Application was therefore made to the Committee, and a new supply, the individual gifts of generous friends of the Tyneside Scottish, soon began to arrive. The dearth of pipers was a serious loss to the Battalions, especially on the march, so that every effort was made to re-establish the pipe bands as quickly as possible. A number of likely volunteers were soon got into training, though, to the uneducated ear, the excruciating sounds which during the course of training issued from secluded spots in the landscape were not particularly soothing. The initiated expressed themselves as satisfied that the result would prove to be everything that could be desired, and I have no doubt that they were right, but pipe playing is an art not learnt in a day, and I, alas, was not destined to listen to the fully re-organised bands. It was while the Brigade was in Divisional reserve at Erquinghem that orders were received for the sudden withdrawal of the Division from the trenches to the back area, so once more we said adieu to Armentieres and without any regrets. The weather had become arctic, and the piercing cold at night in the trenches was terribly trying for the men. The thermometer registered nearly thirty degrees of frost, and sentries found it impossible to keep warm. The move, therefore, was most popular. Our move was *via* Bailleul to the villages in the neighbourhood of Fletre, where Divisional Headquarters were established in an old small château. Our Brigade Headquarters were in a small house in the village of Thieushough, with the various units of the Brigade billeted in farms and villages round about.

The weather was intensely cold but fine, and training was pushed on. Many of the men who formed the drafts lately received by units had had a very short period of training, and had much to learn. Trench life was a special form of soldiering, but it afforded no training for open warfare, and it was therefore important that the troops should be trained to act in the open if, as was hoped, a break through of the enemy's lines should be possible at no very distant date. The training was pushed on accordingly, and the " attack," as in open warfare, was practised daily by all units on the frozen fields in the neighbourhood, which in their present condition allowed of the free movement of troops without any fear of damage to crops. Though every care was always taken by troops to prevent damage when training, a certain amount was almost unavoidable, and in order to deal with this question officers were appointed whose special duty it was to assess damages done. The amount of these damages was a matter of adjustment between the Army authorities and the local mayor, and from the cases which came to my notice on one or two occasions, the peasantry and other owners of property could not complain of want of liberality in this connection. Major Troubridge and I spent much of our time in tramping round visiting Battalions and watching the training. The roads were in places covered with a coat of ice, and the transport had a very hard time of it, though the animals were rough shod. My recollections of this spell are mostly concerned with the intense cold. I abolished every sentry post that was not absolutely essential, and everything, though it was but little, was done for the comfort of the men, and in spite of the weather they were comparatively comfortable.

After about a week we received orders that the

THE RIGOURS OF WINTER

Division was to proceed by march route to Arras, *via* Aire, the Headquarters of the 3rd Army. Before we left his command, General Sir Herbert Plumer paid us a visit of inspection, and as I was for a few days in command of the Division while Major-General Nicholson was temporarily absent, I accompanied the Army Commander on his inspection of the various units. Once more we were on the march, and glad to be on the move again. When passing through Aire the Brigade was subject to a good deal of curiosity from groups of Portuguese soldiers who did not salute, and I'm afraid our men were not greatly impressed by their soldierly appearance. On arrival in the area behind Arras, it was decided that the Division was to go into training, and the Brigades were distributed in villages in the back area accordingly. Our Brigade Headquarters was given a dining-room and two bedrooms in a very nice château in well-kept grounds. The house was inhabited by its owner's representative, a lady, and several servants. The Brigade Staff for the most part were billeted in other houses in the village. The butler, an old servant of the family, did his best to make us comfortable, but nothing would induce him to allow us the use of the front door, which for some unexplained reason was kept locked. The result was that we had to make our entry and exit from the house by means of a long dark passage leading through the domestic offices to the scullery.

Our visitors of high and low military degree had also to adopt this method of approach, and seldom failed to express their surprise at our peculiar arrangements. Our Corps Commander now was Lieutenant-General Sir Charles Fergusson, commanding the 17th Corps, which formed part of the 3rd Army under General Sir E. H. H. Allenby, K.C.B. The ground in the neighbourhood was very suitable for training, and we soon set to work to dig shallow trenches to represent our front line and another for the enemy's front trench. The enemy's communication trenches and reserve trenches were marked out by different coloured flags to represent the actual enemy lines opposite our trenches just north of Arras. Here we used to practise almost daily in conjunction with two aeroplanes. The latter took it in turns to work with us. One of the pilots was a Captain and the other a very youthful Subaltern. They were both killed in aerial fights a short time afterwards. While riding back one day from the attack practice my old horse, Paddy, who had come out from England with me, came down rather badly; he had fallen several times before, so I had regretfully to give him up. He was a good old beast, but, like his master, was not so young as he had been.

We had abominable weather on our march, and one day, after getting a thorough drenching, I was bowled over by an attack of bronchitis, temperature of a hundred and four degrees, and to my disgust was relegated to the nearest hospital. On arriving there in a lorry I failed immediately to find the doctor, who was busy, and decided that if I wanted to see anything of the coming attack at Arras desperate steps must be taken, and that I had better get away at once, so I made a bolt of it, and to the surprise of the hospital orderlies and of the driver, got into the motor lorry again and directed him to pursue and find the Brigade, which, after many wrong directions, was found near St Eloi. I am not quite clear as to what then happened, but I found myself in bed, in a very dilapidated château, and received the greatest attention from a very friendly doctor, a stranger to me. After a day or two I was sufficiently recovered to get moved, I forget how, to a château a few miles away, where I was told Divisional Headquarters had been established, and there met General Nicholson, who, believing me to be in hospital, was much surprised to see

THE RIGOURS OF WINTER 147

me, but my explanation of my somewhat erratic proceedings was accepted, and his good nature was such that he at once agreed to arrange for my being given a room in the château and being attended there by a medical officer, so all was well.

After ten days I was, thanks to General Nicholson's hospitality and the care of the medical officer, practically fit again, and able to rejoin the Brigade, who were in Divisional Reserve in a hut camp just south of St Eloi. These huts were formed of corrugated iron sheets, semi-circular in shape, which formed a tunnel with a door at one end and window at the other. They were a great improvement on tents in wet weather. They had a wooden floor, a table, and an iron stove, and each hut accommodated about twenty men. The mud round the huts was quite up to the average, and the floor of the hut which was utilised as Brigade Headquarters and mess combined had usually a considerable coating of it. The stove when red hot made the temperature impossible, and when it was not red hot the inhabitants suffered from the cold. There is no medium temperature in an army hut. From this camp large working and carrying parties were supplied daily and nightly. St Eloi was a village on rising ground a few miles south of Villers au Bois, our old headquarters when we were holding the Vimy Ridge, and its outstanding feature was a church or monastery with two very high twin towers, which could be seen for miles round. These looked very imposing from a distance, but viewed at close range they were disappointing. The village did not seem to have suffered much from shell-fire, but the towers showed several hits. Arras was six or seven miles to the east of us, and lay in a hollow out of sight. Before the Brigade went into the line I several times went to see General Gore, commanding the 101st Brigade, whom I found occupying a cellar in a brewery in the suburb of St Nicholas, just north of the Scarpe river. Arras had suffered severely from shell-fire; the cathedral was a wreck, and many of the houses were in ruins. The once fine streets of tall houses had a peculiarly melancholy and deserted appearance; a few only of the inhabitants remained, and those lived in their cellars. Troops were billeted in some of the deserted houses, and the occasional movements of a staff motor-car, an ambulance, or small parties of men, or an individual officer rather emphasised the deserted look of the place by day. During the night the movement of transport, working parties and relief troops woke the town up. The road as it approached Arras, being under observation from the Boche lines, was camouflaged with matting hung from tree to tree to form a screen. At the top of the slope leading down to the town is a fine old stone archway under which the road runs. This bit of the road was not, however, one to be lingered on unnecessarily, as it was a favourite target for the Boche, and bodies of troops approaching Arras were, in consequence, diverted from the main road a mile or so in rear. Our Artillery had a battery under cover of some trees near the arch. The Division was at the time holding a length of trench north of the river with one Brigade, the other two being in reserve, and before long we were ordered to move up and relieve the 101st Brigade. The work of forming advanced dumps was similar to that done at Albert, but Captain Marrs was, unfortunately, at this time taken ill, the result of overwork, and was invalided, which entailed the services of Captain H. W. Waller being again requisitioned to act as Staff Captain, assisted by Lieutenant G. S. Pattullo. These officers worked with a will, and there was no hitch. The Brigade moved into the trenches about the last week in March. The Brigade Headquarters of the 101st Brigade had been established in a damp cellar in the suburb of St Nicholas, but I soon came to the conclusion that a few days there would probably result in my once more being attacked by my

THE RIGOURS OF WINTER 149

former enemy, and I persuaded General Nicholson to allow me to move straight away into the dugout in the trenches which we were to shortly occupy when the bombardment, preliminary to the forthcoming attack, should commence. The time taken daily walking up from St Nicholas to the trenches, a distance of a couple of miles, through deep mud was also saved. The experience that we had had at Albert was very valuable to us now; the routine of preparation was similar, though some of the arrangements were not identical. The Brigade was now holding a line of trenches extending from the Scarpe river on the south to a point about a mile northwards. Behind our front lines were the usual supports and reserve trenches, and in rear of the latter the ground rose considerably and formed a ridge, behind which, in a valley, were posted a number of field Artillery batteries.

The village of Roclincourt was about half a mile in rear of the left of our line, and was occupied by one of the Battalions in support. The houses themselves were merely ruins, but some of the cellars were inhabitable. Vimy Ridge, some miles to the north and its continuation to the south, ran opposite to the trenches of the British forces, the ridge gradually decreasing in height until opposite to Arras when it was little more than an undulation, the top of which was about two miles from our lines. The No-Man's-Land lying between our trenches and the Boche lines was about three hundred yards wide, and behind the enemy's front trenches were several other lines of trenches on the sloping ground in the rear. Each trench was heavily protected by barbed wire entanglements. A railway line ran up from Arras through the Boche lines, and by means of a deep cutting crossed the top of the ridge. The last enemy trench ran along the crest, and his field guns were posted just behind the ridge in cemented gun positions. A bridge crossed the railway cutting at the top of the ridge, and, as we subsequently found, under the bridge was a very extensive and elaborate excavation in the northern side of the cutting, which contained a number of rooms forming the headquarters of a Hun Regimental Commander and his staff. On the further side of the ridge the open ground sloped downwards gently to the east, and except for the small village of Bailleul there was nothing in the way of obstruction to the view for about a mile and a half. The general plan of attack included the capture of the Vimy Ridge, and our Division was given the task of attacking the southern spur of the ridge. The northern end of the ridge, the precipitous dominating end, was to be assaulted by the Canadians, who were then occupying the trenches that our two Brigades had held in the summer of 1916. The familiar work of preparing for the attack was pushed along, ammunition, supply, and R.E. dumps were filled, and positions for heavy trench mortars were excavated. Four of these latter were dug out just behind the Brigade Headquarters, and a number of others were placed in the close vicinity of Thelus redoubt. Each of the heavy mortars, known as the " Big Pigs," fired a hundred pound shell, and the slow flight of these projectiles could be easily traced in the air. Their range was about a thousand yards, and their destructive power was enormous. We were quite on a par now with the Hun in this respect, and our Artillery was now so numerous both as regards heavy and light guns, and the supply of ammunition of all kinds was so ample, that the Boche was quite out-distanced, though, of course, he was extremely well equipped.

1. Railway cutting, east of Arras, April, 1917.
2. Bridge over cutting.
3. Entrance to communication trench.   [*To face p.* 150.

CHAPTER XVIII

BATTLE OF ARRAS

We were officially informed by means of a plan of the numbers and position of all our guns, and our concentration of Artillery was up to that time the greatest ever seen. Large numbers of gas mortars, I think four hundred, were one night installed in our lines with a view to drenching a particular point in the enemy's defences with poison gas. The attack was to be on the 9th April, and some few days prior to the date orders were received that the Brigadiers were to attend at General Nicholson's Headquarters to meet the Field-Marshal Commanding-in-Chief. The meeting took place at the château, and in addition to the Commander-in-Chief, the Army Commander, Sir E. H. H. Allenby, K.C.B., and the Corps Commander, Sir Charles Fergusson, were present. The Commander-in-Chief went briefly into the general plan of attack and the enemy's dispositions, and we were each asked for our opinion as to the chances of success. All the Infantry Brigadiers agreed that the scheme was excellent, and that the attack would be successful. Apart from the feeling of absolute confidence in our own men we were also influenced by the knowledge of the immense mass of Artillery which would support the Infantry attack, and the extreme care which had been taken in preparing the details of the Artillery barrage. There was in all ranks a general feeling of confidence, which was amply borne out by the entire success of the subsequent operations. At the end of the interview, which did not last longer than about half an hour, Sir Douglas Haig, having shaken hands and wished us all good luck, drove off accompanied by the Army and Corps Commanders to visit another Division.

The method of attack decided upon for our Division was not identical with that of the 1st July. Instead of, as on the previous occasion, the attack being carried out by two Brigades supported by the third, this time three Battalions of each Brigade were to form the front line of attack, supported by the fourth Battalion of their own Brigades. This latter Battalion was to move forward so as to reinforce the preceding lines upon the latter having reached a certain specified enemy reserve trench, and its start had to be timed accordingly. The Artillery creeping barrage, that curtain of fire which moved in advance of the Infantry, was to be followed up closely by the leading line of the attacking force, and it had been strongly impressed upon all ranks that the success of the attack depended largely upon this point being clearly understood and acted upon. The barrage while falling on an enemy trench effectually prevented the occupants of that trench from maintaining any serious fire on the attacking force, but, of course, it was necessary prior to the actual assault of the trench by the Infantry to "lift" the barrage from off the trench, and when this was done it was essential that our own men should be so close to the trench that they could rush it before the enemy had time to man the parapet and open fire. For this reason the closer our men could follow the barrage the better, the numbers of casualties would be reduced, and the greater the chances of a successful assault. About fifty yards in the rear of the barrage was the extreme limit of safety to our own men from bursting shells, and that this very short distance should have been feasible speaks volumes for the extraordinary pitch of proficiency reached by our Artillery. The accuracy of the gunners was such that the Infantry moving forward just in rear of the barrage could do so with absolute confidence. To

BATTLE OF ARRAS

follow the barrage as closely as possible was half the battle.

The preliminary bombardment on this occasion was somewhat shorter than that preceding the Somme attack, and was to last only three days. Though the volume of sound of this bombardment must have been as great or greater than that produced on the Somme, to us in the trenches it did not appear to be nearly so noisy. No doubt this was due to the fact that the ridge separating the valley in which our guns were posted from the Infantry trenches formed a barrier to the sound. On this occasion four " tanks " had been allocated to the Division, two of them to be attached to our Brigade and two to the 101st. The latter Brigade had one particularly awkward strong point to negotiate which was very heavily wired up and required special treatment, and the tanks were intended to facilitate the Infantry attack by destroying the wire which covered a large area. Our tanks were detailed to assist in our attack generally, but the mud, our inveterate enemy, unfortunately interfered and, as it turned out, the tanks did not get further than the top of the enemy's front line parapet on which they stuck, each balanced on a small mountain of mud. The Brigade Headquarters dugout was situated in a central position about five hundred yards in the rear of our front trench, in what was known as the Thelus Redoubt, a jumble of trenches originally dug by the French. There were three good-sized chambers connected by passages, and each with its own entrance staircase from one of the trenches. The dugouts were about thirty-five feet below the surface, sleeping bunks had been put up, and the accommodation was much superior to that at Albert. This dugout also was dry, which was a great comfort. The preparation for the attack was pushed on vigorously in spite of the mud which in some parts of the trenches was deep and greatly impeded the carriage forward of the trench mortar ammunition. The projectiles for the "Big Pigs" were most difficult to handle, and though an adequate supply did eventually reach the mortar positions a considerable number could not be got up so far, and had to be left in the mud into which they sank out of sight, but no doubt were salved later on. The salvage of derelict articles of all kinds had been instituted at an earlier date, and now was very systematic; every scrap of material that it was possible to make further use of was collected, and either used to supply local requirements or was sent to depots in rear where it was suitably dealt with to the great saving of the taxpayer's pockets.

As Captain Waller's services were now urgently required by his Battalion as a company commander I had regretfully to let him return to his unit, the duties of Staff Captain being carried on by Captain F. Wilson, of the 18th N.F., who, in addition to his other duties, superintended the distribution and adjustment of the trench ladders and bridges. The concentration of the whole of the three Infantry Brigades on the front, which our Brigade was now occupying, took place on the night of the 7th April. The 101st Brigade took over a third of the line on the right, and the 103rd Brigade the third on our left, and we held the central portion. One of the remarkable points which was very noticeable was the evident ignorance of the Boche as to our time-table and arrangements for bringing up the other two Brigades from the rear into the line. While they were moving up, of course, at night, it was fully expected that a considerable fire would be brought to bear on certain points on their line of advance, and dispositions to avoid losses were accordingly made. It was therefore an agreeable surprise to find that the enemy took no notice whatever of the move, and the troops arrived in the trenches having suffered practically no losses in the operation. The Hun Intelligence Department was for once

BATTLE OF ARRAS

seriously at fault. This concentration entailed considerable re-arrangement, for which preparation had been duly made in advance. Our disposition for the attack was the 1st Tyneside Scottish on the right, the 2nd Tyneside Scottish in the centre, and the 3rd Tyneside Scottish on the left, while the 4th Tyneside Scottish was to be in support. The attack was to be carried out in the same Battalion formation as on the 1st July, modified by the adoption of the new system of organisation of platoons under which each section of the platoon consisted of specialists, either bombers, Lewis gunners, etc.

The machine gun company was to support the attack from suitable positions. The preliminary bombardment began on 6th April, and one watched the hammering of the Hun with deep satisfaction. The "Big Pigs," just in rear of our dugout, thoroughly enjoyed themselves, and though the Boche soon discovered their whereabouts and replied with plenty of heavy stuff he never succeeded in dropping a shell quite into any of the mortar pits, which were about ten feet deep and square. A good many of the Boche shells, however, fell on our roof and made big pits in it and in adjoining trenches, and we had each of our three entrances blown in in turn; a certain amount of digging being necessary to clear a way out. One of our men who was acting as mess cook was unfortunately killed, but otherwise the Brigade Staff suffered no casualties. The Boche retaliation was heavy on our trenches, and we had casualties, but on the whole the Brigade got off comparatively lightly. On one of the days of the preliminary bombardment the R.E. let off a salvo of the four hundred mortar gas shells referred to, and expressed themselves as extremely satisfied with the result. The zero hour for the attack was 6.30 a.m. on 9th April, and exactly at that moment the assault was launched on the enemy's front trench, or rather on what remained of it, and from that moment the advance went like clockwork. Messages were regularly received and transmitted to Divisional Headquarters, giving the news of the fall of each of the enemy's trenches in succession, and the final objective, the enemy's last line on the extreme top of the slope, was captured during the afternoon. Several batteries of enemy's guns which they had been forced to abandon were also captured by the Brigade just over the top of the ridge. Similar success attended the attack by the 101st and 103rd Brigades on our right and left, though owing to a temporary check to the troops of another Division on the left of the 103rd Brigade, the latter who had to conform and not lose touch were somewhat delayed in reaching their final objective. The whole operation was remarkably successful, and reflected the greatest credit on the Battalion leaders, officers, and men.

Our losses were comparatively slight, and the enemy's losses in personnel, guns, and material were very considerable. One of the outstanding features of the attack was the skill with which the support Battalion, the 4th Tyneside Scottish, was handled by its Commander, Lieutenant-Colonel C. P. Porch, D.S.O., whose personal gallantry and skilful dispositions had much to do with the success achieved. For his conspicuous gallantry on this occasion he was awarded the rare distinction of a bar to the D.S.O., which he had already gained at Armentieres. All the Battalions did splendidly, and greatly distinguished themselves by the dash and vigour of their attack, and the reputation of the Tyneside Scottish Brigade was more than fully maintained. To my extreme regret, among the officers killed, alas, was Captain H. W. Waller, a serious loss indeed not only to his Battalion, but to the Brigade. Owing to his being from time to time attached to the Brigade Staff one had got to know him well and to value his sterling qualities. Always deeply interested in his work, high principled, greatly liked and re-

BATTLE OF ARRAS

spected by his superior officers and his subordinates as a brave and thoroughly efficient officer, he had made his mark, and his advancement was assured. He met his death while engaged in hunting down an enemy sniper who had been giving trouble on the top of the ridge after the enemy had retired and the battle was over. The capture of the top of the ridge entailed the retreat of the enemy for a considerable distance, though they held on to the village of Bailleul, a few hundred yards to our left front, for two days longer. The village was, however, eventually evacuated, and our patrols were then able to push on down the open sloping country for a distance of over a mile, and reported that the enemy were holding a line of trenches a few hundred yards further on.

All was very quiet, as both sides were moving the bulk of their Artillery, ours forward and the enemy to new positions in their rear. Machine guns opened fire on our patrols as they approached the enemy's new line, and they sent a few shells over our Infantry trenches, aiming more particularly at the communication trenches and the railway cutting bridge, but no serious damage was done. Our men were naturally much elated at their victory, and the commanding officers were full of praise of the splendid performances of their men. There was much to be done to consolidate our new trenches, in getting up ammunition and supplies, and burying the dead. Our Brigade Headquarters moved forward to a dugout in the Boche lines which had been the headquarters of a Hun Company Commander. It was deep underground, and consisted of two rooms with various conveniences in the way of tables, chairs, shelves, and floor covering. The walls were adorned with pictures cut from illustrated papers, and the smaller room was fitted up with sleeping bunks. My servant found among a collection of belongings left by the late owner several dozen of mineral water, which were much appreciated. The captured trenches, especially the enemy's front trench, were so smashed up by our Artillery bombardment that stretches of it were merely irregular mounds of mud. Numerous machine guns were buried in the mud, together with war material of various kinds.

The enemy's existence in the front and support trenches during the bombardment must have been an appalling experience, and prisoners, relating their sufferings, told how impossible it had been for rations and water to reach them during those days, so that hunger and thirst were added to their trouble. Many of the entrances to the dugouts were blown up, and the occupants were in some cases buried alive. The dead and fragments of dead littered the trenches. Lying just outside the entrance to the dugout which I took over were several dead Boche, and at a short distance away was a body of an officer who had lost his life and a leg (evidently blown away by a shell). He was a remarkably good-looking man of about thirty-five, with a Kaiser moustache, and though he lay on his back in a muddy shell-hole his whole appearance was that of a dandy; his smart, well-fitting uniform was evidently quite new, and was absolutely clean, and the ribbon of his iron cross gave a finish to his immaculate appearance. It was evident that he was not a denizen of the trenches, but a staff officer sent down to see and report on the situation. As he lay there with his calm face turned to the sky he looked strangely out of place in the midst of the blood-stained puddles and muck and filth of his surroundings. The capture of the enemy's batteries was a matter of great rejoicing, but at one time it looked as if there might be some trouble in the matter, owing to the fact that apparently the capture of the same battery was claimed by two different Battalions, one of ours and one of the 101st Brigade. The dispute, however, ended happily by the discovery

BATTLE OF ARRAS 159

that it was based upon a misunderstanding; two batteries and not one had been captured, one by each of the claimants, so all was well. On the day following our attack the Canadians, away on our left, who had already captured the Vimy Ridge, carried out an attack on the village of Thelus, about two miles north of Roclincourt, and it was very interesting to watch the progress of this operation. To us following through our glasses the movements of the troops as they moved forward up the slope towards the village, it seemed that the attack was being made by a dense swarm, not lines, of men which slowly but steadily advanced. Numbers of enemy shells were bursting in the mass of men, and frequent gaps were made which, however, soon filled up. Our Artillery was the whole time pouring shells of all calibres into the village, which was enveloped in smoke.

It was a magnificent spectacle, and I regretted that I was unable to stop longer and watch till the end, but other duties prevented, and I missed the final act, the taking of the village. From our position on the top of the ridge we had a very clear open view to the east. The church spire of Gavrelle marked the Boche position on our right front, about two miles away, and the village of Oppy lay a little further off to our left front. Away to the south, Monchez le Preux, the well-known village, perched on the top of a conical hill, showed up very clearly. The Boche seemed to be in no mood to make a counter-attack, and would have received a warm welcome had he attempted to advance up the open slopes which were so covered by our machine guns, as to make such a movement impracticable. On the 14th April the Division was relieved by another, and we marched out of the trenches through Arras to the back area for a rest prior to returning to the line. I myself was to take a longer rest. I had come to the end of my tether, and reluctantly had to acknowledge that there comes a time when one must step aside for a younger man. While arrangements were being made as to my successor, Lieutenant-General Sir Charles Fergusson paid us a visit, and made a congratulatory speech to the Brigade drawn up upon parade, and he was good enough to say pleasant things about myself which I much appreciated. The Brigade, a day or two later, moved to the village of La Thieuloxe, and while it was there I took the opportunity of thanking officers and men for their splendid services and saying good-bye to each Battalion on parade and wishing them good luck. I hated saying good-bye, and as their kindly farewell cheers rang in my ears, one's thoughts went back to all those also of the Brigade, brave comrades of the past, who were calmly sleeping their last sleep not far away. So came to a close my services with the Tyneside Scottish Brigade, indeed a gallant company with whom it was my great privilege to have been so closely associated. It was with very sincere regret that I made my adieux to General Nicholson, that best and most considerate of chiefs, and the Divisional Staff who had been such good friends to us all in difficult times. The subsequent doings of the old Brigade will be, no doubt, chronicled in due course; my task is done; my wife, who has acted as typist and critic, has cheered me by stating that in her opinion my attempt at telling the tale is " Not at all bad." I do not suggest that such high praise is really merited, but still it encourages one to hope that this little narrative will not be altogether without interest to any friends of the Brigade into whose hands it may fall.

---

www.ingramcontent.com/pod-product-compliance
Lightning Source LLC
Chambersburg PA
CBHW031144160426
43193CB00008B/246